The Family Meal

Home cooking with Ferran Adrià

From elBulli to your kitchen

—

What is the family meal?

The family meal is the dinner eaten every day by the 75 members of staff at elBulli restaurant. We call it that because the staff members are like a family, and the family meal is an important moment when everyone sits down together to eat. You might assume that the staff would eat the same food as the guests, but they don't. In fact, people are often surprised when we tell them that we eat ordinary food.

Why is the family meal so important at elBulli? The answer is very simple: we believe that if we eat well, we cook well.

WHY THIS BOOK?

This book is the result of three years' work by Eugeni de Diego (one of the head chefs, and responsible for the family meal) and Ferran Adrià, who created and planned the recipes together. We thought it would be a shame for all this work to end up gathering dust in a drawer. Once we knew that elBulli would close on 30 July 2011, we decided to collect all the family meal recipes into a book. At first, we thought only professionals would be interested. Restaurants around the world feed their staff every day, and we hoped we could contribute to our profession by offering varied and nutritionally balanced menus for large numbers.

But then we thought: why not offer our philosophy to home cooks too? Domestic cooks can learn many tips from how things are organized in a professional kitchen, and *The Family Meal* aims to show people how easy it can be to cook in an organized way, by adapting our recipes for home cooks.

It was never our intention to invent brand-new recipes; this is simply a collection of everyday varied and inexpensive meals. It is a book about simple cooking. We wanted to showcase ordinary recipes for dishes that people might imagine are difficult to make, such as vichyssoise or chocolate cookies. The food we like to eat at elBulli is the same as what most people like to eat.

You don't need experience to follow the recipes, as each recipe is explained step by step. In fact, what is presented here is more a way of thinking about food than a way of cooking. We truly believe that if you don't eat well, it's because you haven't tried.

RECIPES OR MEALS?

There are many recipe books, but very few based on meals. People often pick up a cookbook at home, but have no idea how to combine the recipes into a sensible meal. This book aims to help by providing meals that have been thought out in their entirety. They have been organized into thirty-one balanced menus, each one containing three courses. You can also make your own menus by combining the recipes using the list on page 65.

WHAT WAS THE THINKING BEHIND EACH MEAL?

It is a myth that good food has to be expensive, and all the recipes in this book were designed to feed people very well on a low budget. Of course, the price will not be the same everywhere in the world.

Shopping in a supermarket is not the same as shopping in a market, just as shopping in Barcelona is different from doing it in Birmingham, New York or Melbourne. However, the principle is still the same: it's about planning and cooking reasonably priced meals with locally available ingredients. Secondly, each meal contains a starter, main course and dessert. Thirdly, the menus are practical. In general, the thirty-one meals offer a healthy, balanced diet with an interesting variety of ingredients and cooking methods.

The ingredients are, for the most part, everyday ones that can be found anywhere in the world, and are not expensive. To make sure of this, one of the chefs at elBulli spent thirty-one days cooking all the meals for two people, buying all the necessary ingredients at the market or supermarket. If he couldn't get hold of them easily, that particular menu was rejected. And whenever possible, we have suggested substitute ingredients.

The elBulli staff eat the same food as in many Spanish homes. However, given that we have staff members of many nationalities, other dishes and methods of preparation have been introduced, for example from Mexico and Japan. But the ingredients required for these recipes can still be found nearly everywhere.

Although most of the recipes use only fresh ingredients, we don't object to using frozen foods when it makes sense, for example in the case of peas, which are more expensive when fresh, have a short season and are almost the same quality when frozen. It's also important to make good use of the freezer when preparing large quantities of basic recipes, such as stocks or sauces, in advance (see page 40).

–

The elBulli system

–

PRODUCTION SHEETS

Planning a different meal every day for 75 people can't be left to chance. At elBulli, we have a system of procedures to make the task easier, which has been perfected over time. First, the recipe is recorded and the details are updated on a production sheet. This means that the dish is always made the same way, regardless of who is in the kitchen and how many people need to be fed. Twice or three times a year, we prepare large batches of the basic recipes (such as sauces or stocks) to freeze and use when needed, dividing them into convenient portions.

MONTHLY AND WEEKLY SHEETS

Each month we make up a menu sheet, showing what is going to be eaten every day of the following month, with special attention paid to variety, rotation, season and availability of ingredients. On the last day of each week the monthly sheet is used to confirm the sheet for the following week. This is only changed if something out-of-the-ordinary happens, such as when a supplier brings us an unexpected ingredient. All of this monthly and weekly planning is done by Eugeni and Ferran.

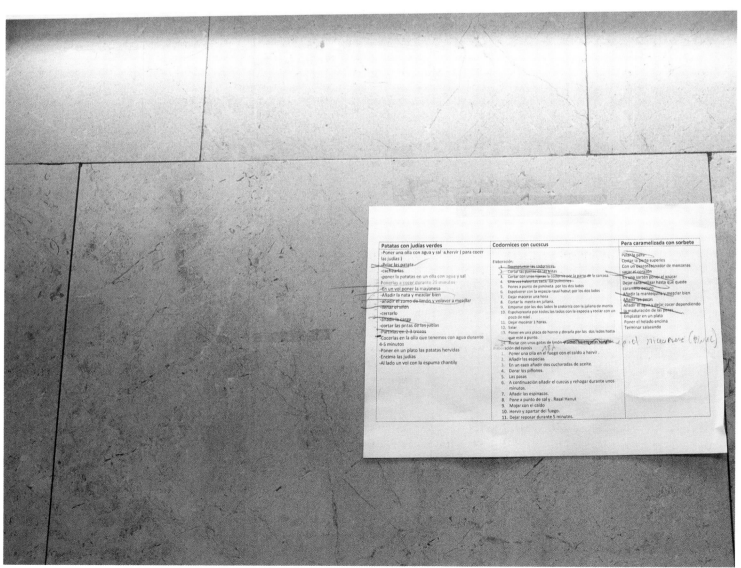

DAY TO DAY

The night before each meal is to be prepared, we check our ingredients are to hand, unless they must be bought fresh on the day, which is the case with fish. On the day itself, between 2.00 pm and 6.25 pm, the work of the *mise en place* (or preparation for that night's service) is alternated with preparing the family meal. It is rare for something to be prepared the day before; this would only apply to a dish such as a special stew.

The *mise en place* for the restaurant dishes is complete by 6.25 pm. At this point we clear the work surfaces, arrange the chairs and put out bottles of water, glasses and bread ready for the family meal. In the meantime, the rest of the chefs and waiting staff line up to collect the first course, which is served in the kitchen. The main course is usually placed on the table on big platters that we call *violines* ('violins'). The dessert is usually served separately (in individual servings or on platters) and it can be collected before or after the main course. Bread is always served with the meal. After trying several different varieties, we decided to serve sliced country loaves, because there is less wastage than with rolls or baguettes. Any unused bread is kept for the following day or used in a dish.

QUANTITIES, PLATTERS AND BOWLS

The recipes in this book are given for 2, 6, 20 or 75 people. The quantities have been carefully calculated to yield the correct amount for each number of people; it's not as simple as straightforward multiplying or dividing. We don't plate each dish individually when cooking for 75 people, but often serve food on platters instead, allowing the staff to take the amount they want. Over time we have worked out how much food is really needed, adjusting the production sheets as we repeated the recipes. Leftover food can be recycled or reused. Side dishes and salads are served in small bowls for the same reason, enabling us to cook more accurate quantities. Of course, when cooking at home for 2 or 6 this is less of a concern, and it is easier to calculate quantities precisely.

STAFF PREFERENCES

The staff have their favourite dishes; in fact, they aren't all that different from the preferences of people who don't work in a cutting-edge restaurant. We noticed, for instance, that staff members took more second helpings of fresh pasta than of other dishes. So we started to make it in larger quantities, allowing everyone to have a second serving. Another staff favourite is rice in any form: black rice, risotto, rice stew. Among the main courses, hamburgers are always high on the list of favourites.

COFFEE AND CLEAR-UP

When the staff have finished their meal, they clear away their plates, glasses and cutlery, and have a coffee. Every day, a member of the waiting staff takes it in turn to make coffee for everybody. In the end, only Ferran is left at the table. He has a brief meeting with Eugeni to deal with anything that has cropped up during the meal. The chairs are cleared away at 7.00 pm. After a few minutes' rest, it's time to get back to work.

TRICKS TO MAKE THE MOST OF INGREDIENTS OR PREPARATIONS

One of the most useful resources of professional kitchens are the ingredients or preparations left over from the *mise en place,* which can be used when making the staff meal. Here are some tips that we have developed at elBulli. Naturally, the individual character and style of each restaurant means it will have its own ingredients and preparations that it can use in different ways.

* After making almond milk, the almond pulp can be saved for use in *ajo blanco* (a traditional Spanish garlic and almond soup), or ice cream.

* After making cheese water, especially with Parmesan, the leftover fat can be used in a risotto.

* If we need the loin of a mackerel (or any other specific part of a fish) for the restaurant, the rest can go to make soup, tartare or fishcakes.

* After using asparagus tips, the stalks can be boiled and served with mayonnaise, or made into a soup, purée or crème.

* Fruit that is too ripe to be served, and leftover pieces of fruit, can be used in sorbets and fruit sauces.

* After making olive water, the olive pulp can be used in soup or for vinaigrette.

* The leftover pulp from making coconut milk can be used in desserts such as macaroons and coconut crème caramel.

* After making tomato water (for water ice, for example), the leftover pulp can be used for *sofrito* or tomato sauce. This operation can also be reversed: if the pulp is needed, the leftover water can be made into a refreshing drink.

* When making stock, the remaining solids can be simmered again with fresh water. The resulting liquid (which we call the 'second stock') is used instead of water the next time we make stock, making it tastier.

* When making chicken stock, the chicken meat can be shredded for use in a salad.

* When making ham stock, the leftover scraps of ham can be made into a dish with peas.

* When using egg yolks, the whites can be saved for another dish (a mousse or meringue, for instance). When using egg whites, the yolks can go into an egg yolk and caramel pudding.

These are some of the many options that can provide tasty and interesting dishes, as well as helping you use leftover food more efficiently and save money.

THE MAGIC THICKENER

For many years it has been common practice for restaurant professionals to use xanthan gum, a hydrocolloid with great thickening power, for binding and thickening sauces, among other things. It's a very effective product: just the tiniest amount can be used to replace traditional thickeners such as cornflour. This is also significant for flavour; as so little xanthan gum is used, it doesn't affect the taste of the dish at all. For these reasons it makes sense to use xanthan gum in professional kitchens. However, the quantities needed at home would be very small and difficult to measure. If you are cooking for a few people at home, it's easier to thicken a sauce or vinaigrette with cornflour by making a paste with a liquid and stirring it into the sauce, heating until it thickens. If you are cooking for 75 people this operation would be difficult to do with cornflour. In this case, a tiny and very precise quantity of xanthan gum gives a perfect result.

THE CRU TECHNIQUE   The technique we call 'CRU' at elBulli consists of vacuum sealing an ingredient that contains a good proportion of liquid (a fruit or vegetable, for instance) along with a liquid with another flavour and aroma. The surrounding liquid from the outside penetrates the ingredient, replacing its own liquid and flavouring it. Some examples of this are apple with Calvados, pineapple with fennel, apple with basil, artichoke with vinaigrette, and asparagus with Parmesan water.

–

Cooking at home

–

ORGANIZATION COMES FIRST   While we were adapting the family meals to be made easily at home, we realized how important the *mise en place* (or advance preparation) is for restaurants. At home, of course, people don't usually prepare in advance. But *mise en place* can be very helpful, even at home. There are always things that need doing on the same day, but there are other things such as stocks and sauces that can be made in advance. Practical concerns will dictate what you can do in advance – the most important thing is to make efficient use of your time. First, it's useful to plan your meals for the week and make a list of everything you can buy in advance (the freshest ingredients will have to wait until the actual day). Following the 'Organizing the Menu' instructions at the beginning of each of our thirty-one meals will enable you to prepare the three courses in very little time. Leave the more complex menus or the ones requiring longer preparation times for the weekend.

SHOPPING   Is it better to shop at a market or a supermarket? Both have their critics and fans, and their advantages and disadvantages. Markets and small private shops allow you to become familiar with the suppliers, so that direct contact and confidence can build up. Many people place great value on knowing their butcher and fishmonger. When buying meat or seafood, they take advantage of these professionals' experience and leave the preparation to them, including the most tiresome operations such as scaling, boning, gutting, chopping, and so on. They can also offer good advice on the most suitable meat cuts or types of fish for a specific recipe. Supermarkets, on the other hand, often offer lower prices because they buy in bulk. Don't forget that you can also do your shopping over the internet. Many large supermarkets offer this service, which helps you to shop efficiently, especially for items to fill the pantry. In the end, the best idea is to combine all the options, and to shop however it suits you.

FRUIT AND VEGETABLES   It's always best to give priority to fruit and vegetables that are in season. Bear in mind that the price of fruit and vegetables is always higher at the start of the season than at its height. Compare prices and always choose the most reasonably priced ones. You can buy them in small quantities and use them as you need.

DAIRY PRODUCTS Buy products made with whole milk, as the percentage of fat in them makes them more suitable for many of the dishes in this book. When buying cream, it's important to know if it's for whipping or cooking. The different kinds have a different fat content, so always read the information on the package. Yoghurt is an excellent product because it has so many possibilities. There are many varieties with different chacteristics such as flavour, creaminess, sweetness and fat content. When it comes to choosing yoghurt for cooking, it's best not to complicate matters: good-quality full-fat plain yoghurt is the best option.

BREAD Bakeries nowadays sell fresh bread in all shapes and sizes. You can also find ready-to-bake or par-baked baguettes and different kinds of pre-packaged loaves. Follow your preferences, but bear in mind how it can be bought and stored. Remember that you can freeze bread and defrost it quickly in the oven or toaster.

OIL You can buy oil of many different qualities and at varying price levels. The menus in this book require three basic types of oil: ordinary olive oil for cooking, extra-virgin olive oil for dressings and sunflower oil for frying.

FISH Try to develop a personal contact at the fishmonger's. It's helpful to talk to someone you can trust and who knows the characteristics of the different species of fish, to help you make the best choices.

The quickest way to test whether fish is fresh is to look at its eyes and skin. The eyes should be black, shiny and convex; if they are grey or look flat or sunken, the fish is past its best. The skin should be shiny and firm; if it's dull or wrinkled, it isn't fresh. Smell can also help you to determine whether fish is fresh. It shouldn't smell; if it does, it should smell more of the sea than of fish. A strong fishy smell means it isn't as fresh as it should be. When storing fish in the fridge, use a plastic container with a lattice tray to separate the fish from the liquid it releases.

When buying fish for home use, ask the fishmonger to gut and scale it for you. You can also ask for the fish to be skinned and filleted, if you prefer.

Pages 16–17 contain photographs of the fish used in the book. Unlike vegetables or meat, one fish can look quite similar to another, so it is helpful to know what you are looking for before you go shopping. If you can't find the fish specified in the recipe, ask your fishmonger to suggest a suitable alternative.

–
MEAGRE
–

Lime-marinated fish
(see page 152)

–
COD
–

Salt cod & vegetable stew
(see page 104)
Cod & green pepper sandwich
(see page 292)

–
HORSE MACKEREL
–

Mackerel with vinaigrette
(see page 164)

–
WHITING
–

Whiting in salsa verde
(see page 233)

–
SEA BASS
–

Lime-marinated fish
(see page 152)
Japanese-style bream
(see page 194)
and *Baked sea bass*
(see page 332)

SARDINE

–

Sesame sardines with carrot salad
(see page 114)

MEGRIM

–

Fried fish with garlic
(see page 252)

MACKEREL

–

Mackerel & potato stew
(see page 84)

BLUE WHITING

–

Whiting in salsa verde
(see page 233)

GILTHEAD BREAM

–

Japanese-style bream
(see page 194)

MEAT   Price is an essential consideration when buying meat, since it can be a very expensive ingredient. However, there is fantastic scope for making high-quality and varied meat dishes using cheaper cuts. Some meats, such as free-range chicken, turkey, duck, pork and certain veal and beef cuts, are quite affordable. Remember that it's always better to buy a good-quality cheap cut than a poor example of an expensive one. You can always make an exception and choose a good sirloin steak every now and again. When it comes to buying meat, you can buy it pre-cut and packaged, or ask the butcher to cut it up in front of you, in which case the meat will be fresher. The same is true of minced meat: you can buy it packaged (even as ready-to-cook hamburgers) or ask the butcher to grind it for you on the spot, allowing you to specify how fine you would like it.

HOW TO COOK MEAT   Every kind of meat needs its own cooking technique and temperature. However, as a general guideline, follow the four principles of what we call the 'heat equation':

1.   the intensity of the heat should be high
2.   the amount of oil should be minimal
3.   the pan should be thick: the thicker the pan, the better the heat will be distributed over the surface, as the entire surface does not come into direct contact with the heating element or gas flame
4.   the quantity of meat should be proportionate to the pan surface area. If you put too much meat in a small frying pan, it will lose a lot of heat. For the same reason, it's best to take the meat out of the fridge 30 minutes before you start cooking.

SIDE DISHES   There are many different side dishes that can accompany meat, including the following:

*   grilled vegetables, such as courgettes, potatoes or bell peppers
*   boiled vegetables, such as cauliflower, potatoes or cabbage
*   baked or roasted vegetables, such as potatoes or courgettes
*   fried vegetables, such as onion rings or aubergine slices
*   pulses, such as beans or chickpeas
*   salads, which could include vegetables, nuts, meat or cheese, such as Waldorf salad (page 370) or Caesar salad (page 72)
*   rice, such as plain boiled rice or Mexican rice (page 242)
*   other dishes that appear as starters in this book, such as Roasted vegetables with olive oil (page 350), Polenta and Parmesan gratin (page 112), Grilled lettuce hearts (page 360), Creamed potatoes (page 362), or Cauliflower with béchamel (page 260)

HOW TO MAKE CHIPS

We have not included chips in any of the menus in this book, but many people consider them the perfect accompaniment to meat dishes. To make the best chips, cut, wash and dry the potatoes, then blanch them quickly in plenty of hot oil (140°C/285°F) in a deep-fat fryer. They shouldn't change colour at this stage. You can do this in advance, then set the chips aside on kitchen paper to drain, keeping them at room temperature. Just before serving, fry them in very hot oil (180°C/360°F) until golden and crisp.

HOW TO COOK EGGS

Some of the dishes in this book can be accompanied with an egg. There are many ways to cook this versatile ingredient, and there are many ways to use it: by itself, in a hot or cold soup, in a salad, or to accompany cooked chickpeas, to name just a few.

To check whether an egg is fresh, immerse it in water. If it stays horizontal at the bottom of the receptacle, it's fresh. If the larger end rises, it's not fresh, and the higher it rises the less fresh it is. If it floats, you should throw it away.

The simplest and most popular way of cooking eggs is to fry them and add to salads, soups or other dishes. You can also use soft-boiled eggs for the same purpose, cooking them in boiling water for 3 minutes so that the inside is still runny.

Another classic method is poaching, which involves immersing an egg in very hot water until the white surrounding the yolk is set.

Finally, there is a wonderful way to cook eggs known in Japan as *onsen tamago*. This originally meant cooking eggs in hot springs with a temperature of 60–70°C (140–160°F). The same technique can be used in restaurant kitchens using a Roner (a low-temperature water bath) or a steam oven set to 63°C (145°F), and cooking the eggs for 40 minutes.

The following page shows the most common techniques for cooking eggs.

1. **Frying**
    Crack the egg into a small bowl before pouring it carefully into the frying pan. Make sure the pan is very hot before adding the egg. If you are serving the eggs in a salad or soup, you can trim off most of the white with a cookie cutter for a neater presentation.

2. **Boiling**
    Make sure the water is fully boiling and have a timer handy when you immerse the egg. Boil for 3–4 minutes for a soft-boiled egg and 7 minutes for a hard-boiled egg. Place immediately in iced water, then peel carefully.

3. **Poaching**
    Crack the egg into a small bowl before pouring it carefully into the water. Make sure the water is just below boiling point and gently slide the egg in. Cook for 3–4 minutes, then remove with a slotted spoon. The yolk should be runny inside.

Frying →

Boiling →

Poaching →

20

HERBS, SPICES AND CONDIMENTS

Herbs are a very useful ingredient in any kitchen, as a relatively small amount allows you to modify the flavour of a dish. If you only need small quantities, you can grow a few pots of the most commonly used herbs in or near your kitchen. This requires basic care, including watering, careful pruning, and so on, but it's economical and the best way to have ready access to the goodness of fresh herbs. It's like having a living pantry. Alternatively, you can buy packets of fresh herbs at the supermarket. You can also generally find large bunches of fresh herbs in markets, which is especially useful when you need larger quantities.

FRESH HERBS

The fresh herbs used in the recipes in this book are:

* parsley
* coriander
* mint
* basil

* thyme
* rosemary
* chives

DRIED HERBS

Another way to add flavour and aroma is to use dried herbs, a practical option available all year round. There is also a long tradition of using dried herbs. The following dried herbs are used in our recipes:

* oregano
* bay leaves

* thyme
* rosemary

SPICES, SAUCES AND CONDIMENTS

No other ingredient has as much power to enhance flavour and aroma as spices. For many centuries they were considered precious commodities for precisely this reason. Spices are also easy to store in a pantry. Even so, it's best to buy them only in small quantities; if you keep them in the cupboard for months or even years, they lose their aroma and freshness. Like spices, condiments can have an important influence on flavour, and can give preparations and dishes an unmistakable quality.

The following spices and condiments appear in this book:

* cinnamon
* cloves
* saffron
* black pepper
* white pepper
* sweet paprika
* nutmeg
* fresh ginger
* red miso paste
* soy sauce
* dashi
* yellow curry paste
* achiote paste
* red *mole* paste

* vanilla
* green anise
* cumin
* five-spice powder
* *ras el hanout* (a Moroccan spice mix)
* *sichimi togarashi* (a Japanese spice mix)
* chilli
* Dijon mustard
* Worcestershire sauce
* oyster sauce
* wholegrain mustard

Using spices and condiments is a very appealing way to experiment with your cooking. If you dare to invent, change and modify, each spice will impart a distinctive flavour to your cooking.

STORING FOOD AT HOME

Minced meat can spoil more quickly than whole meat cuts, as it has a larger surface area in contact with the air. When storing meat in the fridge, discard the bags or paper wrapping from the shop and transfer to plastic containers with lids, in order not to mix smells and to prevent the cold air from drying out the meat. Once the packaging of a product is opened, the period for its safe use varies depending on the type of food and the temperature at which it is stored. As a general rule, an opened fresh product can safely be stored for two or three days at the correct temperature. Always transfer the contents of open cans to other (non-metallic) containers.

Fruit and vegetables can lose their nutritional properties once they have been cut or sliced, so use them quickly after preparing them. Don't store vegetables in plastic bags or other wrapping that can shorten their life.

The recipe quantities have been carefully calculated to avoid wastage. If there are any leftovers, however, they can be stored in the fridge for a few days.

FREEZING FOOD

Label everything you want to freeze, and include the date of freezing. Frozen food should be well packed to preserve its properties and to prevent it from taking on other smells. Freeze ingredients and preparations in small portions, bearing in mind the quantities you are likely to need for the recipes. Defrost and clean your freezer regularly to ensure it is working efficiently. Every type of food has a different freezer life, but it is generally unwise to keep food in the freezer for longer than 6 months. Not all ingredients can withstand freezing in the same way. For example, peas and beans barely suffer any reduction in quality, but the same is not true of artichokes and courgettes. Remember to take things out of the freezer the day before you want to use them. Thaw meat or fish by leaving it on a plate, covered, in the fridge.

KITCHEN EQUIPMENT

To make the meals in this book you will need only basic kitchen utensils and equipment. The most essential equipment is listed on pages 24–25, and further useful, but not essential, equipment is listed on pages 26–27.

1. Large and small kitchen knives

2. Kitchen scissors

3. Wooden spoons

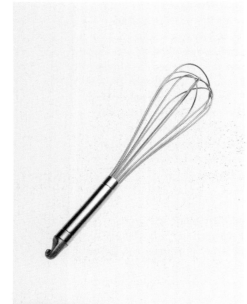

4. Balloon whisk

5. Spatula

6. Mortar and pestle

7. Grater

8. Non-stick frying pan

9. Large, medium and small saucepans

10. Ovenproof dishes

11. Measuring jug

12. Fine-meshed sieves

13. Pepper mill

14. Kitchen paper

15. Aluminium foil

16. Clingfilm

17. Baking parchment or greaseproof paper

18. Moulds of different sizes

19. Squeezy bottles

20. Lemon squeezer

21. Pasta machine

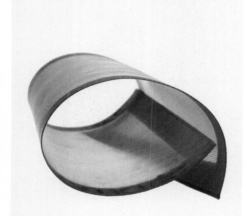
22. Non-stick baking mat

23. Mandolin

24. Microplane grater

25. Flat griddle

26. Casserole dish

27. Pressure cooker

28. Kitchen blowtorch

29. N₂O siphon and cartridges

30. Soda siphon

31. Electric scale

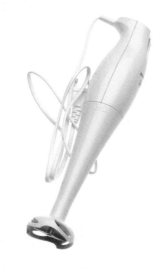

32. Hand-held blender

33. Electric lemon squeezer

34. Electric fruit and vegetable juicer

35. Blender

36. Food processor

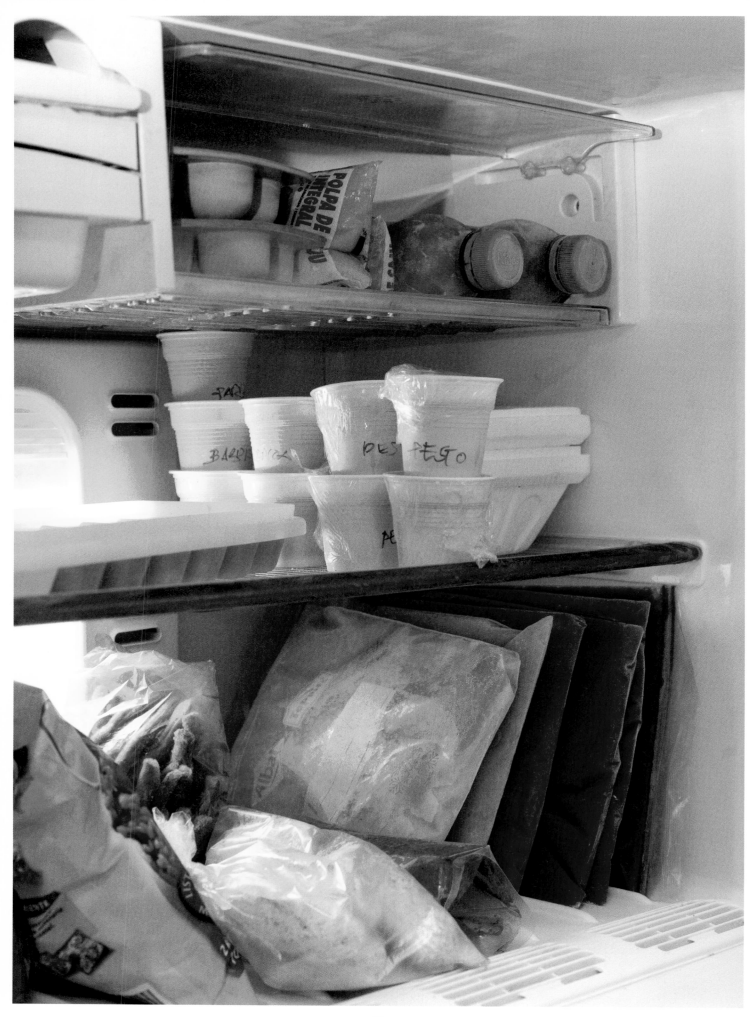

The essentials

—

A good pantry should be well stocked with ingredients with a relatively long shelf life. Start by buying a few of these basic ingredients now, and complete the list as you prepare the menus. By the time you have cooked all the recipes you will have built up a very good basic pantry.

Store all fresh ingredients in the fridge. The freezer is an ideal place to store freshly made preparations such as stocks and sauces, for use in different menus over a period of several months.

FRIDGE
* eggs
* butter
* wholemilk
* whipping cream (35% fat)
* Parmesan cheese
* cheese slices
* plain yoghurt
* smoked bacon
* Frankfurter sausages
* limes
* lemons
* other citrus fruits
* apples
* oranges

FREEZER
* fish stock (see page 56)
* chicken stock (see page 57)
* beef stock (see page 58)
* ham stock (see page 59)
* picada (see page 41)
* tomato sauce (see page 42)
* sofrito (see page 43)
* bolognese sauce (see page 44)
* romesco sauce (see page 45)
* pesto sauce (see page 46)
* peas
* spinach
* nougat ice cream
* vanilla ice cream
* squid ink

PANTRY

HERBS, SPICES AND FLAVOURINGS
* five-spice powder
* green anise seeds
* saffron
* ground cinnamon
* cloves
* ground cumin
* dried chillies
* ground nutmeg
* achiote paste
* dashi powder
* *ras el hanout*
* *sichimi togarashi* spice mix
* sweet paprika
* table salt
* sea salt flakes
* white pepper
* black pepper
* vanilla pods
* dried bay leaves
* dried oregano
* dried rosemary
* dried thyme

VEGETABLES
* garlic
* onions
* potatoes

OILS AND VINEGARS
* sunflower oil
* ordinary olive oil
* extra-virgin olive oil
* toasted sesame seed oil
* sherry vinegar
* white wine vinegar
* red wine vinegar

PRESERVED INGREDIENTS

* pickled capers
* tinned coconut milk
* pickled gherkins
* tinned cooked beans
* tinned cooked lentils
* tinned anchovy fillets
* tinned or bottled tomato sauce
* tinned sweetcorn
* chopped tomatoes
* dried shiitake mushrooms

STARCH

* rice
* couscous
* polenta
* tagliatelle
* spaghetti
* short egg noodles
* farfalle
* macaroni
* egg noodles
* white caster sugar
* icing sugar
* brown sugar
* honey
* molasses
* cornflour
* ground almonds
* plain white flour
* corn tortillas
* croutons (see page 52)
* potato flakes

SAUCES AND CONDIMENTS

* mayonnaise
* red miso paste
* black olive paste
* red *mole* paste
* wholegrain mustard
* Dijon mustard
* barbecue sauce (see page 48)
* oyster sauce
* soy sauce
* teriyaki sauce (see page 50)
* Worcestershire sauce

ALCOHOL

* brandy
* Cointreau
* Cognac
* kirsch
* anisette liqueur
* white rum
* white wine
* Chinese Shaoxing rice wine
* *vino rancio* (or dry sherry)
* red wine

NUTS AND SEEDS

* caramelized almonds
* whole toasted Marcona almonds
* caramelized hazelnuts
* prunes
* crushed almonds
* peeled walnuts
* raisins
* pine nuts
* peeled green pistachio nuts
* white sesame seeds
* toasted white sesame seeds

OTHER PRODUCTS

* potato crisps
* potato straws
* dark chocolate
* white chocolate
* cocoa powder
* instant coffee
* grated coconut
* menthol throat sweets
* honey-flavoured boiled sweets
* N_2O siphon cartridges

A look behind
the scenes at the
family meal

—

The following pages provide a glimpse of the restaurant before it opens its doors. These are the precious minutes between preparation and service: a time to sit down, talk, enjoy a coffee, and, of course, to eat.

First, the work surface is cleared and the plates are set out; then the staff begin to queue to collect their meal from the kitchen. Platters of food are set out along the table and everyone sits down together in the kitchen to eat.

Finally, the tables are cleared and the work surfaces are made ready for the beginning of the restaurant service.

Basic recipes

Basic recipes

The basic recipes are for base preparations such as sauces and stocks that are used in the meals that follow, and preparing them in advance will make it easier for you to cook in a more organized way. In fact, the main difference between cooking at home and cooking professionally lies in the level of advance preparation (or *mise en place*) that happens in restaurants. Restaurant chefs make large batches of basic stocks, sauces and garnishes ahead of time, to make cooking both staff meals and restaurant dishes simpler and quicker. These preparations are sometimes vacuum packed before freezing, but at home it's fine just to freeze them.

Think of the basic recipes as your *mise en place* on a domestic scale. We recommend that you set aside time to prepare your basic recipes, and to make the largest possible quantities (depending on the size of your pans and freezer), to make it worth your while. By having these preparations to hand at any time, you can greatly expand your repertoire of delicious everyday dishes.

The amounts that the basic recipes will yield are given in grams or millilitres, rather than serving numbers, because different recipes will require different quantities. It is simple to multiply the recipes up or down to prepare the quantity you need. When making stocks, it's best to make as much as you can, then store in smaller quantities in the freezer to use as you need. Ice-cube trays and small plastic cups or re-sealable food storage bags are excellent for storing small portions of preparations, such as *picada*, *sofrito* or pesto, and plastic bottles or airtight containers are ideal for storing stock. Remember that liquids expand as they freeze, so always allow a little room in the top of the bottle or container. Always label the preparation clearly with the name, quantity and date of freezing.

Of course, good alternatives to these stocks and sauces can be bought from any good supermarket or delicatessen. What you choose to use will depend on the time you have available and the amount you want to spend. When buying ready-made stocks and sauces, always look for the best quality you can afford. There are a number of alternatives to making your own stock, as explained in the following pages, and another good option is to buy several litres of stock from a restaurant that you trust.

To make this way of cooking work for you, it's important to remember to take whatever you need from the freezer the day before.

Picada

–

Picada is an aromatic sauce traditionally used in Catalan cuisine as a base flavouring for many dishes. It is also often added towards the end of cooking.

•

Picada will keep for 1 week in the fridge or 6 months in the freezer.

•

This sauce appears in:
Beans with clams (page 102)
Crab & rice stew (page 204)
Black rice with cuttlefish (page 272)
Fish soup (page 320)
Rice with duck (page 342)
Salmon stewed with lentils (page 352)
Noodle soup with mussels (page 372)

	for 100 g	for 500 g
Saffron threads	0.5 g	2.5 g
Fresh parsley leaves	25 g	125 g
Garlic cloves	1 clove	30 g
Extra-virgin olive oil	40 ml	200 ml
Toasted blanched hazelnuts	35 g	175 g

Start →

Wrap the saffron threads in aluminium foil and toast lightly in a hot frying pan for a few seconds, taking care not to let them burn. Cool.

Put the peeled garlic and the parsley leaves into a small bowl.

Add the toasted saffron threads.

Next, add the olive oil.

Process with a hand-held blender to make a coarse paste.

Add the toasted hazelnuts and continue to process to make an even, fine mixture.

Tomato sauce

The sauce will keep for 5 days in the fridge or 6 months in the freezer.

•

This sauce appears in:
Sausages with tomato sauce (page 144)
Ossobuco (page 154)
Spaghetti with tomato & basil (page 250)

	for 230 g	for 2.3 kg	for 8 kg
Extra-virgin olive oil	120 ml	1.2 l	4 l
Garlic cloves	½	25 g	75 g
Onions, finely chopped	1 tsp	175 g	500 g
Tinned chopped tomatoes or passata	350 g	3.5 kg	12 kg
Salt	1 pinch	30 g	100 g
Pepper	1 pinch	6 g	20 g
Sugar	1 pinch	30 g	100 g

Start →

Put a large saucepan over a high heat, then add the oil. Fry the garlic for a few seconds.

Add the onion and cook for 5 minutes.

Add the tomatoes and simmer until they have reduced by one-third.

Add the salt, pepper and sugar.

Pass the sauce through a fine-meshed sieve.

Sofrito

Sofrito is a basic preparation of tomatoes, garlic, oil and onions that forms the basis of many traditional Spanish dishes.

•

The sauce will keep for 5 days in the fridge or 6 months in the freezer.

•

This sauce appears in:
Beans with clams (page 102)
Crab & rice stew (page 204)
Black rice with cuttlefish (page 272)
Fish soup (page 320)
Rice with duck (page 342)
Salmon stewed with lentils (page 352)
Noodle soup with mussels (page 372)

	for 100 g	for 350 g	for 1 kg
Garlic cloves	1	40 g	140 g
Extra-virgin olive oil	2 tsp	120 ml	400 ml
Onions	300 g	1 kg	3.2 kg
Dried thyme	1 pinch	1 g	3 g
Dried rosemary	1 pinch	1 g	3 g
Dried bay leaf	⅛ leaf	½ leaf	1.5 g
Puréed fresh tomatoes or passata	1½ tbsp	225 g	800 g
Salt	1 pinch	2 g	8 g

Start →

Put the garlic into a tall jug or beaker, then process to a paste using a hand-held blender.

Put a saucepan over a medium heat and add the oil. Fry the garlic until browned.

Meanwhile, process the onion in the blender. Add to the pan with the garlic.

Lower the heat, add the herbs, then fry, stirring frequently, until the onion has browned.

Add four-fifths of the tomatoes and cook for 30 minutes.

Add the remaining tomato, cook for 30 more minutes, then season with salt and pepper.

Bolognese sauce

The sauce will keep for 5 days in the fridge or 6 months in the freezer.

•

If you prefer to cook it in the oven, cover the sauce with a lid or foil and cook for 1½ hours at 180°C/365°F/Gas Mark 4.

•

This sauce appears in:
Pasta bolognese (page 82)

	for 2.5 kg	for 8 kg
Butter	225 g	800 g
Minced beef	1.2 kg	4 kg
Pork sausage meat	350 g	1.3 kg
Onions	500 g	1.75 kg
Celery	150 g	500 g
Carrots	400 g	1.5 kg
Extra-virgin olive oil	150 ml	500 ml
Tomato purée	12 g	40 g
Tinned chopped tomatoes	1.6 kg	5.25 kg
Sugar	1 pinch	2 g

Start →

Put a large pan over a medium-high heat, then add the butter and let it melt. Add the beef mince, fry until it has changed colour, then add the sausage meat.

Cook for a few more minutes, season with salt and pepper, then cook for 15 minutes longer, stirring frequently, until dark golden brown.

Meanwhile, finely chop the onions and celery. Finely chop the carrots.

Put another pan over a low heat, then pour in the olive oil. Fry the vegetables gently until softened, about 12 minutes.

Add the meat to the vegetables and mix everything together well.

Add the chopped tomatoes and the tomato purée. Season with salt, pepper and sugar. Simmer the sauce for 1½ hours until the meat is very tender.

Romesco sauce

Romesco is a traditional Catalan sauce made with nuts and peppers pounded with oil and sherry vinegar. It is usually served with seafood, chicken or vegetables. *Choricero* pepper paste is available from specialist Spanish food shops and delicatessens.

•

The sauce will keep for 5 days in the fridge or 6 months in the freezer.

•

This sauce appears in:
Baked potatoes with romesco sauce (page 232)

	for 5 kg	for 15 kg
Ripe tomatoes	350 g	750 g
Garlic, whole heads	150 g	400 g
Extra-virgin olive oil	300 ml	900 ml
Toasted blanched hazelnuts	350 g	1 kg
White country-style loaf, sliced	1 kg	1.7 kg
Sherry vinegar	2.5 l	8 l
Choricero pepper paste	1.2 l	4.5 l

Start →

Preheat the oven to 200°C/400°F/Gas Mark 6. Put the whole tomatoes and heads of garlic into a roasting tin and cook for 45 minutes, or until blackened and tender.

When cool enough to handle, peel the tomatoes and put into a bowl.

Cut away the top of the garlic heads, then squeeze the softened flesh into the bowl with the tomatoes.

Put the pan over a medium heat, add a little oil, and fry the hazelnuts for 4–5 minutes until dark golden. Drain the nuts on kitchen paper.

Fry the bread in a little more oil, then drain on kitchen paper. Tear the bread into pieces.

Put the nuts, torn-up bread, vinegar and choricero paste into the bowl then season with salt and pepper. Process with a hand-held blender to make a coarse paste.

Blend in the remaining oil until smooth.

Pesto sauce

–

Pesto will keep for 2 days in the fridge or 6 months in the freezer.

•

This sauce appears in:
Farfalle with pesto (page 192)

	for 1.6 kg	for 6 kg
Fresh basil	425 g	1.6 kg
Garlic cloves	25 g	100 g
Pine nuts	120 g	435 g
Extra-virgin olive oil	190 ml	700 ml
Olive oil	425 ml	1.6 l
Pecorino cheese, finely grated	50 g	200 g
Parmesan cheese, finely grated	230 g	870 g

Start →

Pick the basil leaves from the stems, discarding any that are damaged.

Bring a saucepan of water to the boil, then add the basil leaves.

Leave in the water for 5 seconds, until wilted.

Drain in a sieve, then when cool enough to handle, squeeze dry and set aside.

Cut each garlic clove in half. Fill a small saucepan with cold water, then add the garlic. Bring the pan to the boil.

Lift the garlic out of the water and transfer to a bowl of iced water to cool.

Roughly chop the basil.

Put the basil, pine nuts, blanched garlic and both types of olive oil into a large bowl.

Process with a hand-held blender to make a coarse and grainy sauce.

Stir the cheeses into the sauce. Season with salt.

Transfer into small containers for storage.

Barbecue sauce

The sauce will keep for 1 week in the fridge or 6 months in the freezer.

•

Molasses is a thick, dark syrup. If you cannot find it, treacle can be substituted.

•

This sauce appears in:
Pork ribs with barbecue sauce (page 262)

	for 1.5 kg	for 5 kg
Red onions	1.2 kg	4 kg
Garlic cloves	15 g	50 g
Lemongrass	30 g	100 g
Fresh root ginger	65 g	250 g
Oranges	450 g	1.5 kg
Golden granulated sugar	270 g	900 g
Runny honey	120 g	400 g
Molasses	120 g	400 g
Sherry vinegar	150 g	500 g
Dijon mustard	60 g	200 g
Worcestershire sauce	15 g	50 g
Tomato ketchup	800 g	3 kg
Tinned chopped tomatoes	1.2 kg	4 kg

Start →

Roughly chop the onions.

Using a rolling pin or other heavy utensil, crush the garlic cloves, lemongrass and ginger, then finely chop them.

Squeeze the oranges and reserve the juice.

Put a large saucepan over a medium heat, then add the oil. Add the onion and cook for 5 minutes, until dark golden.

Add the garlic and cook for 3 minutes more.

Add the brown sugar, orange juice and molasses and let the mixture cook for 3 minutes.

Continue →

Pour in the honey.

Add the ginger and lemongrass.

Add the mustard, Worcestershire sauce and ketchup.

Add the tomatoes and simmer for 30 minutes.

Season with salt.

Strain through a fine-meshed sieve and leave to cool.

Teriyaki sauce

The sauce will keep for 15 days in the fridge or 6 months in the freezer.

•

This sauce appears in:
Glazed teriyaki pork belly (page 302)

	for 1 kg	for 4 kg
Lemongrass	75 g	200 g
Fresh root ginger	30 g	100 g
Chicken stock (see page 57)	400 ml	1.5 l
Soy sauce	400 ml	1.5 l
Sugar	600 g	2 kg
Runny honey	400 g	1.5 kg

Start →

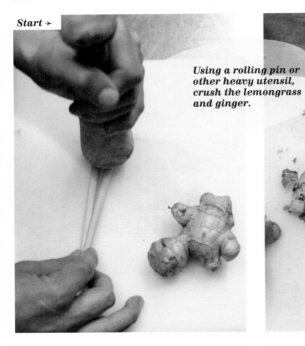

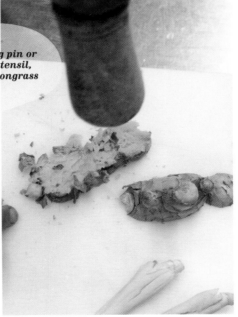

Using a rolling pin or other heavy utensil, crush the lemongrass and ginger.

Put the chicken stock, sugar, and soy sauce into a large saucepan.

Add the honey.

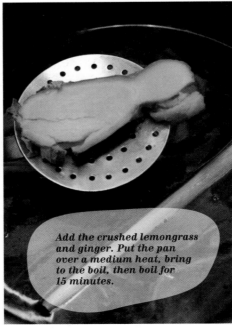

Add the crushed lemongrass and ginger. Put the pan over a medium heat, bring to the boil, then boil for 15 minutes.

Strain and reserve.

Chimichurri sauce

Chimichurri is a sauce made from parsley, garlic, spices, olive oil and vinegar. It comes from South America, where it is often served with steak, but it can accompany all types of roasted or grilled meat.

•

The sauce will keep for 15 days in the fridge and 6 months in the freezer.

•

This sauce appears in:
Duck with chimichurri sauce (page 226)

	for 3.5 l	for 7 l
Onions	375 g	750 g
Garlic	100 g	200 g
Fresh parsley	150 g	300 g
Ripe tomatoes	1.5 kg	3 kg
Small chillies	2	4
Dried thyme	5 g	10 g
Dried oregano	25 g	50 g
Ground cumin	2 g	5 g
Sweet paprika	12 g	25 g
Coarse salt	35 g	75 g
Lemons	1	2
Sherry vinegar	125 g	250 g
Chardonnay vinegar	250 g	500 g
Olive oil	750 g	1.5 l
Sunflower oil	500 g	1 l
Water	750 g	1.5 l

Start →

Chop the onions and garlic very finely, then put into a large bowl. Pick the parsley leaves from the stems and chop finely. Add to the bowl.

Deseed and cut the tomatoes into small cubes. Deseed and finely chop the chillies. Mix both into the onions and garlic and stir in the herbs and spices. Finely grate in the zest of the lemons.

Finish by pouring in the vinegars, oil and the water.

Croutons

This recipe is for fried croutons, but if you prefer to toast the croutons, preheat the oven to 170°C/375°F/Gas Mark 5. Spread the croutons out over a baking tray and bake for 8–10 minutes.

•

This recipe appears in:
Caesar salad (page 72)
Vichyssoise (page 92)
Gazpacho (page 270)
Fish soup (page 320)

	for 100 g	for 400 g
Slices from a white country-style loaf	3	20
Extra-virgin olive oil	500 ml	1 l

Start →

Cut the bread into 1.5-cm squares.

Put a deep pan over a medium heat, then add the oil.

When the oil is hot, fry in the cubes in batches for 6–8 minutes until golden brown and crisp.

Lift the croutons out of the oil with a slotted spoon.

Transfer onto kitchen paper, and leave to drain.

Serve warm or cold.

Aïoli

Aïoli is a thick mayonnaise-like sauce from southern France made with garlic, eggs and oil.

•

This sauce appears in:
Mackerel & potato stew (page 84)
Crab & rice stew (page 204)
Black rice with cuttlefish (page 272)

	for 1.5 l
Garlic cloves	5
Eggs	8
Extra-virgin olive oil	1.25 l

Start →

Peel the garlic cloves.

Cut each garlic clove in half, and remove the central pale green sprout from the garlic, if there is one.

Put the eggs and garlic into a high-sided bowl or beaker.

Process with a hand-held blender until smooth.

With the blender running, add the oil little by little. Season with salt.

The aïoli should have a thick, creamy texture like mayonnaise.

Stock

–

Wherever stock appears in a recipe, you can use ready-made concentrated or fresh liquid stock, or home-made stock.
A concentrated cube produces an instant stock when dissolved in boiling water. Many chefs prefer not to use this kind of stock, but it is a valid option for the home cook, with the advantages of being cheap and easy to use. The flavour of the stock can sometimes be enhanced with meat or yeast concentrates, if needed. Ready-made liquid stock is available in the form of a concentrated liquid for diluting, or a fully diluted stock that has been prepared naturally, then packed. The latter is the better choice although it is also more expensive. The third option – making the stock at home following the recipes we provide – involves the most effort, but will give you the best quality results.

The quantity of stock you can make at home will be limited by the size of pans in your kitchen: the largest domestic pans usually have a capacity of around 9 litres. Filled with plenty of good ingredients, a 9-litre pot will yield approximately 6 litres of stock, which can later be frozen in 500-ml portions, ready for use. The idea that stock needs a lot of time and attention is unfounded; it takes just 20 minutes to cook fish stock, and up to 2½ hours will be long enough for most meat stocks. Once a stock is simmering, it can be left to cook while you do something else. After straining a meat stock, don't throw the bones and other ingredients away. They can be re-boiled for 45 minutes, and the liquid from this second boiling (which we call the 'second stock'), can be used instead of water when making the next batch of stock to give it a deeper flavour. Fish bones cannot be re-boiled, as they become bitter.

Fresh stock will keep in the fridge for up to 2 days, or in the freezer for up to 3 months.

Fish stock

—

Fish stock can be made with a mixture of any white fish and crustaceans, and crabs are a very good addition.

•

This stock is used in the following recipes:
Mackerel & potato stew (page 84)
Beans with clams (page 102)
Crab & rice stew (page 204)
Black rice with cuttlefish (page 272)
Salmon stewed with lentils (page 352)
Noodle soup with mussels (page 372)

	for 3 l
Olive oil	25 ml
Crabs	400 g
Fish	1.7 kg
Water	4 l

Start →

Put a very large saucepan over a medium heat, then add the olive oil. Add the crabs. Cook for 3–5 minutes.

Add the fish.

Pour in the water and bring to a simmer.

Skim the foam from the surface.

Simmer for 20 minutes, then strain through a fine-meshed sieve.

Cool before putting into containers.

Chicken stock

–

This stock is used in the following recipes:
Vichyssoise (page 92)
Saffron risotto with mushrooms (page 132)
Bread & garlic soup (page 212)
Chickpeas with spinach & egg (page 300)
Rice with duck (page 342)

	for 2 l
Onions	130 g
Carrots	80 g
Celery	40 g
Whole, cleaned, raw chicken carcasses	1.25 kg (4 carcasses)
Water	5 l

Start →

Cut the onions in half. Put the carrots, onions, celery and chicken carcasses into a very large saucepan.

Pour in the water, then bring to the boil.

Skim the foam from the surface.

Simmer for 2½ hours.

Remove the chicken and vegetables and strain through a fine-meshed sieve.

Beef stock

This stock is used in the following recipes:
Ossobuco (page 154)

	for 2 l
Onions	130 g
Beef off-cuts or cheap pieces of meat, such as shank	1 kg
Beef bones, raw	2.7 kg
Carrots	80 g
Celery	40 g
Water	5 l

Start →

Cut the onions in half. Put the beef and bones in a very large saucepan with the carrots, onions and celery.

Pour in the water and bring to the boil.

Skim the foam from the surface.

Simmer for 2½ hours.

Strain through a fine sieve. Cool before putting into containers.

Ham stock

This recipe requires the bones from a cured ham. Ask your butcher to supply them. Remove any meat from the bones and use in another recipe.

•

<u>This stock is used in the following recipes:</u>
Peas & ham (page 280)

	for 2 l
Ham bones	1.35 kg
Water	4 l

Start →

Remove most of the meat from the ham bones. Put the bones into a very large saucepan.

Pour in the water and bring to the boil.

Skim the foam from the surface.

Simmer for 1½ hours.

Strain through a fine-meshed sieve.

Cool and skim away any fat from the surface before putting into containers.

The meals

Meals & Recipes

Meal 1

Caesar salad

Cheeseburger & potato crisps

Santiago cake

Meal 2

Pasta bolognese

Mackerel & potato stew

Chocolate cookies

Meal 3

Vichyssoise

Lamb with mustard & mint

Chocolate truffles

Meal 4

Beans with clams

Salt cod & vegetable stew

Baked apples

Meal 5

Polenta & Parmesan gratin

Sesame sardines with carrot salad

Mango with white chocolate yoghurt

Meal 6

Crisp omelette

Pork loin with peppers

Coconut macaroons

Meal 7

Saffron risotto with mushrooms

Catalan-style turkey

Yoghurt foam with strawberries

Meal 8

Roast aubergine with miso dressing

Sausages with tomato sauce

Crème Catalane

Meal 9

Lime-marinated fish

Ossobuco

Piña colada

Meal 10

Miso soup with clams

Mackerel with vinaigrette

Almond biscuits

Meal 11

Fried egg with asparagus

Chicken wings with mushrooms

Sangria with fruit

Meal 12

Potato salad

Thai beef curry

Strawberries in vinegar

Meal 13

Farfalle with pesto

Japanese-style bream

Mandarins with Cointreau

Meal 14

Tomato & basil salad

Crab & rice stew

Coconut flan

Meal 15

Bread & garlic soup

Mexican-style slow-cooked pork

Figs with cream & kirsch

Meal 16

-

Noodles
with shiitake
& ginger

-

Duck with
chimichurri
sauce

-

Pistachio
custard

-

Meal 17

-

Baked potatoes
with
romesco sauce

-

Whiting
in
salsa verde

-

Rice pudding

-

Meal 18

-

Guacamole with
tortilla chips

-

Mexican-style
chicken with rice

-

Watermelon
with
menthol sweets

-

Meal 19

-

Spaghetti
with
tomato & basil

-

Fried fish
with
garlic

-

Caramel
foam

-

Meal 20

-

Cauliflower
with
béchamel

-

Pork ribs
with
barbecue sauce

-

Banana
with lime

-

Meal 21

-

Gazpacho

-

Black rice
with
cuttlefish

-

Bread
with chocolate
& olive oil

-

Meal 22

-

Peas & ham

-

Roast chicken
with
potato straws

-

Pineapple
with
molasses & lime

-

Meal 23

-

Tagliatelle
carbonara

-

Cod &
green pepper
sandwich

-

Almond soup
with
ice cream

-

Meal 24

-

Chickpeas
with
spinach & egg

-

Glazed teriyaki
pork belly

-

Sweet potato
with
honey & cream

Meal 25

-

Potatoes &
green beans
with Chantilly

-

Quails
with couscous

-

Caramelized
pears

Meal 26

-

Fish soup

-

Sausages
with
mushrooms

-

Oranges with
honey, olive oil
& salt

Meal 27

-

Mussels
with
paprika

-

Baked
sea bass

-

Caramel
pudding

Meal 28

-

Melon
with
cured ham

-

Rice
with duck

-

Chocolate
cake

Meal 29

-

Roasted vegetables
with olive oil

-

Salmon stewed
with lentils

-

White chocolate
cream

Meal 30

-

Grilled lettuce
hearts

-

Veal with
red wine
& mustard

-

Chocolate
mousse

Meal 31

-

Waldorf salad

-

Noodle soup
with
mussels

-

Melon & mint soup
with
pink grapefruit

How to choose and
prepare for the meals

1.   Choose a menu, considering factors such as the amount of time you have available and the preferences of your guests. Check the Organizing the Menu timeline first. Most of the meals take between 30 minutes and 2 hours to make all three dishes. The most time-consuming recipe is usually the dessert. If you leave out dessert, preparation times rarely exceed 30 minutes.

2.   Read the recipes, ingredients lists and the Organizing the Menu timeline carefully.

3.   Study the shopping lists to check which ingredients you already have.

4.   Buy the ingredients you need.

5.   Follow the recipe carefully.

Create your own menu

Although the recipes have been carefully designed to form complete meals, you can combine the recipes in different ways to create new meals or to avoid certain dishes that you or your guests may not like. Use this list to help you choose recipes for different types of dish and compile your own menu, resulting in a more varied and balanced meal.

COURSE	TYPE OF DISH	RECIPE	PAGE	MEAL
Cold starters	Salads	Lime-marinated fish	152	9
		Potato salad	182	12
		Caesar salad	72	1
		Tomato & basil salad	202	14
		Melon with cured ham	340	28
		Waldorf salad	370	31
	Soups	Gazpacho	270	21
		Vichyssoise	92	3
	Vegetables	Guacamole with tortilla chips	240	18
Warm starters	Rice & pasta	Tagliatelle carbonara	290	23
		Spaghetti with tomato & basil	250	19
		Farfalle with pesto	192	13
		Pasta bolognese	82	2
		Noodles with shiitake & ginger	222	16
		Polenta & Parmesan gratin	112	5
		Saffron risotto with mushrooms	132	7
	Eggs	Fried eggs with asparagus	172	11
		Crisp omelette	122	6
	Pulses	Chickpeas with spinach & egg	300	24
		Beans with clams	102	4
	Soups	Miso soup with clams	162	10
		Bread & garlic soup	212	15
		Fish soup	320	26
	Shellfish	Mussels with paprika	330	27
	Vegetables	Roasted aubergine with miso dressing	142	8
		Grilled lettuce hearts	360	30
		Cauliflower with béchamel	260	20
		Roasted vegetables with olive oil	350	29
		Peas & ham	280	22
		Baked potatoes with romesco sauce	232	17
		Potatoes & green beans with Chantilly	310	25

COURSE	TYPE OF DISH	RECIPE	PAGE	MEAL
Desserts	*Fruit*	*Mandarins with Cointreau*	*197*	*13*
		Mango with white chocolate yoghurt	*116*	*5*
		Baked apples	*106*	*4*
		Oranges with honey, olive oil & salt	*324*	*26*
		Caramelized pears	*314*	*25*
		Piña colada	*157*	*9*
		Pineapple with molasses & lime	*284*	*22*
		Banana with lime	*264*	*20*
		Watermelon with menthol sweets	*245*	*18*
		Sangría with fruit	*176*	*11*
		Melon & mint soup with pink grapefruit	*374*	*31*
	Others	*Rice pudding*	*235*	*17*
		Yoghurt foam with strawberries	*136*	*7*
		Almond biscuits	*166*	*10*
		Coconut macaroons	*126*	*6*
		Santiago cake	*76*	*1*
		Caramel pudding	*334*	*27*
		Sweet potato with honey & cream	*304*	*24*

—

Meal 1

—

Caesar salad

—

Cheeseburger
&
potato crisps

—

Santiago cake

INGREDIENTS

BUY FRESH
* Romaine, Cos
  or iceberg lettuce
* minced beef
* burger buns
* fresh burger toppings,
  such as onions
  or tomatoes
* lemons

IN THE CUPBOARD
* garlic
* anchovy fillets
  in olive oil
* sherry vinegar
* sunflower oil
* salt
* white peppercorns
* olive oil
* croutons (see page 52)
* potato crisps
* pickles or condiments
  to go with the burgers
* flour
* sugar
* ground almonds
* ground cinnamon
* icing sugar

IN THE FRIDGE
* Parmesan cheese
* whole milk
* eggs
* cheese slices
* butter

–
Caesar salad
–

–
*Cheeseburger
&
potato crisps*
–

70

Santiago cake

	Hours before the meal
	4
	3½
	3
	2½
2 hours before Make the Santiago cake and leave to cool	2
Make the burgers and keep in the fridge	1½
	1
30 minutes before Make the Caesar dressing and wash the lettuce	½
Turn the cake out of the baking tray, slice and dust with icing sugar	
5 minutes before Cook the burgers	
Just before eating Finish the Caesar salad and put in a serving dish	
Toast the burger buns and make up the cheeseburgers to your taste	
	Start of the meal

Caesar salad

To make your own croutons,
see page 52.

•

Mild olive oil can be used instead
of sunflower oil, and Cos
or Iceberg lettuce can be used
instead of Romaine.

•

The secret of a good Caesar salad is
to use good ingredients and to dress
the salad at the last minute.

	for 2	for 6	for 20	for 75
For the dressing:				
Garlic cloves	½	1½	4	12
Anchovy fillets packed in olive oil, drained	2	6	40 g	140 g
Egg yolks	1	2	3	12
Sherry vinegar	2 tsp	2 tbsp	8 ml	30 ml
Sunflower oil	3 tbsp plus 1 tsp	200 ml	600 ml	1.5 l
Parmesan cheese, finely grated	20 g	40 g	120 g	300 g
For the salad:				
Romaine lettuce	1 small head	1½ heads	2 kg	7.5 kg
Croutons	30 g	50 g	300 g	1 kg
Parmesan cheese, finely grated	20 g	60 g	150 g	500 g

Start →

Put the garlic, anchovies and egg yolks into a tall jug or beaker.

Process with a hand-held blender until smooth.

Very gradually pour in the sunflower oil while blending to make a smooth, thickened sauce that looks similar to mayonnaise. Blend in the vinegar.

Stir in the grated Parmesan.

Continue →

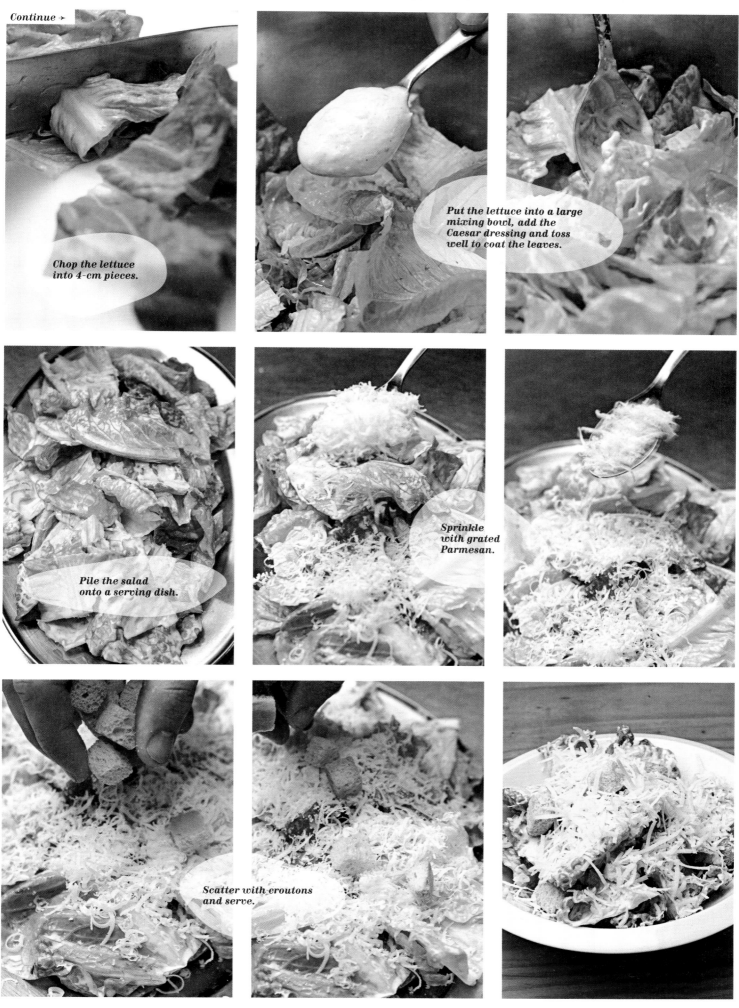

Chop the lettuce into 4-cm pieces.

Put the lettuce into a large mixing bowl, add the Caesar dressing and toss well to coat the leaves.

Pile the salad onto a serving dish.

Sprinkle with grated Parmesan.

Scatter with croutons and serve.

Cheeseburger & potato crisps

To make it even easier, you could use good-quality ready-made burger patties. If making your own, look for good-quality beef chuck with about 10% fat.

•

You can add any other toppings you like, such as onion, tomato, pickles, mustard, ketchup and mayonnaise. To make a caramelized onion topping, thinly slice some onions and cook very gently with a little oil for about 1 hour, until soft and golden.

	for 2	for 6	for 20	for 75
White bread (crusts removed)	7 g	20 g	65 g	250 g
Whole milk	1½ tsp	20 ml	65 ml	250 ml
Minced beef	250 g	660 g	2.2 kg	8 kg
Eggs	½	1	4	15
Salt	¼ tsp	1 tsp	22 g	80 g
Freshly ground white pepper	1 pinch	¼ tsp	6 g	20 g
Burger buns	2	6	20	75
Olive oil	2 tbsp	6 tbsp	400 ml	1.5 l
Cheddar cheese slices	2	6	20	75
Potato crisps	50 g	150 g	500 g	2 kg

Start →

To make the burgers, tear the bread into pieces and soak in the milk for 5 minutes.

Combine the meat, eggs, soaked bread, salt and pepper in a large bowl.

Stir together with your hands until you have an even mixture.

Shape into burgers weighing about 135 g each – one per person.

Continue →

Cook the burgers with the oil in a frying pan over a medium heat, or under a hot grill, turning once during cooking.

Cook for 3 minutes for rare, 5 minutes for medium and 8 minutes for well done.

Cut the buns in half and toast them lightly in a dry pan or under the grill.

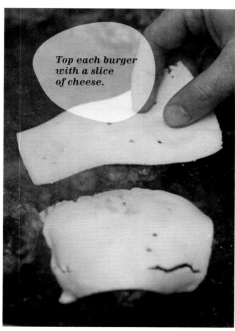

Top each burger with a slice of cheese.

Using a spatula, lift each burger onto a bun.

Sandwich with the top half of the bun.

Add your choice of toppings.

Serve the burgers with potato crisps on the side.

Santiago cake

This traditional almond cake originated in the Spanish city of Santiago de Compostela in the 16th century.

•

The cake can be flavoured with dessert wine or port. Add 2 tbsp when you fold in the ground almonds.

•

We do not recommend making less than the quantity given for one cake, which will serve 12 people. Any leftover cake will keep in an airtight container for up to 4 days.

	for 2	for 12 (one cake)	for 20	for 75
Butter	–	1 tbsp	10 g	30 g
Flour	–	1 tbsp	10 g	30 g
Large eggs, 70 g each	–	3	6	22
Sugar		150 g	300 g	1 kg
Ground almonds		150 g	300 g	1 kg
Ground cinnamon	–	1 pinch	1.5 g	5 g
Lemons	–	½	1	2
Icing sugar	–	1 tbsp	30 g	90 g

Start →

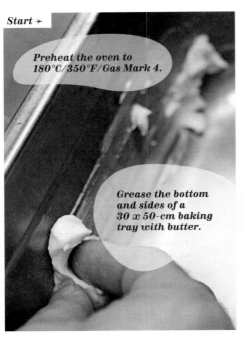

Preheat the oven to 180°C/350°F/Gas Mark 4.

Grease the bottom and sides of a 30 x 50-cm baking tray with butter.

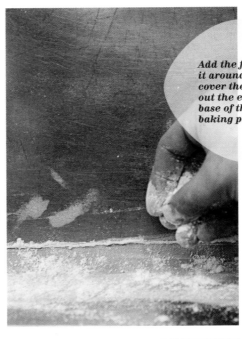

Add the flour and tap it around the tray to cover the butter. Tip out the excess. Line the base of the tray with baking parchment.

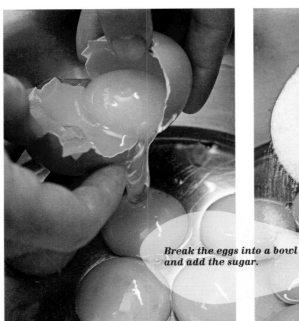

Break the eggs into a bowl and add the sugar.

Using a free-standing mixer or an electric hand whisk, beat the eggs and sugar until thick and foamy, about 5 minutes.

Continue →

Mix the ground almonds with the cinnamon.

Finely grate in lemon zest, then stir until evenly mixed.

Add the ground almond mixture to the eggs and sugar. Fold in carefully with a spatula to retain as much air as possible.

Pour the mixture into the prepared tray.

The cake mixture should be about 1.5 cm deep.

Bake in the oven for 17 minutes, or until evenly risen, golden and shrinking away from the sides of the tray. Remove from the oven and leave to cool in the tray.

Remove the cake from the tray and cut into portions.

Sprinkle icing sugar over the top using a fine-meshed sieve before serving.

–

Meal 2

–

Pasta bolognese

–

Mackerel & potato stew

–

Chocolate cookies

INGREDIENTS

BUY FRESH
* mackerel
* ripe tomatoes
* fresh parsley
* new potatoes

IN THE CUPBOARD
* garlic
* salt
* pasta
* extra-virgin olive oil
* olive oil
* mild paprika
* black peppercorns
* cornflour
* vanilla pods
* sugar
* dark chocolate,
  75% cocoa
* white chocolate
* flour
* five-spice powder
* instant coffee

IN THE FRIDGE
* Parmesan cheese
* aioli (see page 53)
* eggs
* butter

IN THE FREEZER
* bolognese sauce
  (see page 44)
* fish stock (see page 56)

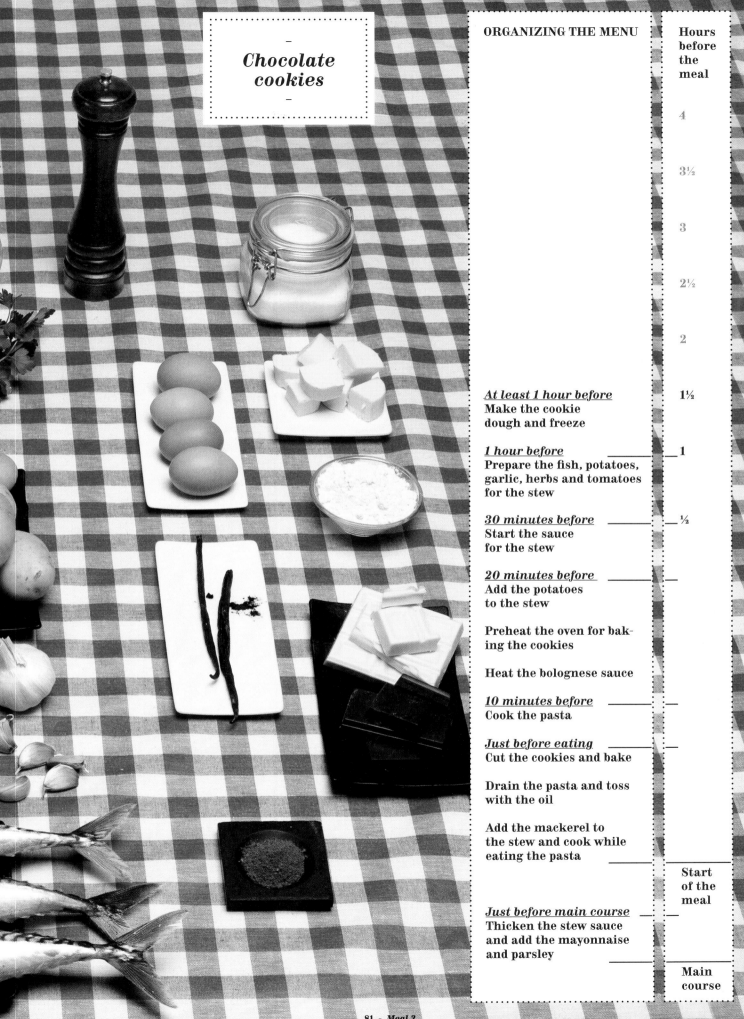

ORGANIZING THE MENU

	Hours before the meal
	4
	3½
	3
	2½
	2
<u>*At least 1 hour before*</u> **Make the cookie dough and freeze**	1½
<u>*1 hour before*</u> **Prepare the fish, potatoes, garlic, herbs and tomatoes for the stew**	1
<u>*30 minutes before*</u> **Start the sauce for the stew**	½
<u>*20 minutes before*</u> **Add the potatoes to the stew**	
Preheat the oven for baking the cookies	
Heat the bolognese sauce	
<u>*10 minutes before*</u> **Cook the pasta**	
<u>*Just before eating*</u> **Cut the cookies and bake**	
Drain the pasta and toss with the oil	
Add the mackerel to the stew and cook while eating the pasta	
	Start of the meal
<u>*Just before main course*</u> **Thicken the stew sauce and add the mayonnaise and parsley**	
	Main course

Pasta bolognese

Bolognese sauce (see page 44)
can be made ahead and frozen.
Do not forget to defrost it in advance.

•

You can use any kind of pasta for
this dish. In Italy bolognese sauce is
traditionally eaten with tagliatelle.

	for 2	for 6	for 20	for 75
Bolognese sauce (see page 44)	175 g	540 g	2 kg	7.5 kg
Water	1.5 l	3 l	6 l	22 l
Salt	3 tsp	30 g	60 g	220 g
Penne pasta	180 g	540 g	1.8 kg	7 kg
Extra-virgin olive oil	3 tbsp	120 ml	400 ml	1.5 l
Parmesan cheese, finely grated	60 g	180 g	600 g	2 kg

Start →

Put the bolognese sauce into a large pan over a medium heat.

Bring to a simmer, stirring occasionally.

Bring the water to the boil in a large pan, season with the salt, then add the penne.

Stir once, then boil the pasta for 8–10 minutes (check the instructions on the packet) until tender but still firm to the bite.

82

Continue →

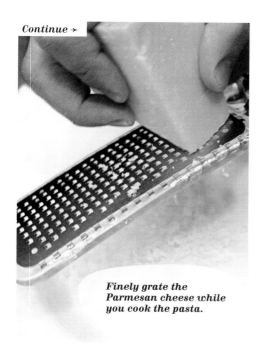

Finely grate the Parmesan cheese while you cook the pasta.

Drain the pasta.

Tip it back into the pan and stir in the olive oil to prevent it sticking together.

Serve the pasta topped with a large spoonful of bolognese sauce.

Serve the Parmesan cheese separately for everyone to sprinkle their own.

Mackerel & potato stew

This dish is a *suquet*, a traditional Catalan fish stew with a simple sauce of tomatoes, paprika and parsley.

•

Ask your fishmonger to clean and gut the fish for you if you prefer.

•

You can use picada (see page 41) or mayonnaise instead of the aioli if you like.

•

The combination of garlic, oil, parsley and tomato makes a kind of instant sofrito.

	for 2	for 6	for 20	for 75
Mackerel, 350 g each	1	3	10	38
New potatoes	250 g	750 g	2.5 kg	9 kg
Garlic cloves	2	5	50 g	150 g
Fresh parsley, finely chopped	1½ tbsp	3 tbsp	85 g	325 g
Tomatoes, coarsely grated	1½ tbsp	4 tbsp	1 kg	4 kg
Olive oil	1½ tbsp	3 tbsp	250 ml	700 ml
Sweet paprika	1 tsp	3 tsp	50 g	180 g
Fish stock (see page 56)	400 ml	1.2 l	4 l	12 l
Cornflour	1 tsp	2 tsp	80 g	250 g
Aioli (see page 53)	½ tsp	1 tsp	100 g	300 g

Start →

Cut the head and tail off the mackerel.

Cut along the belly of the fish and remove the insides using your hands or a spoon.

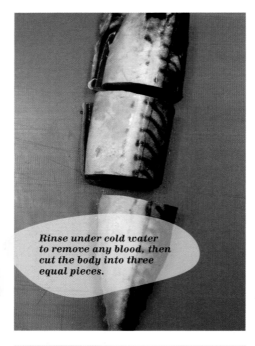

Rinse under cold water to remove any blood, then cut the body into three equal pieces.

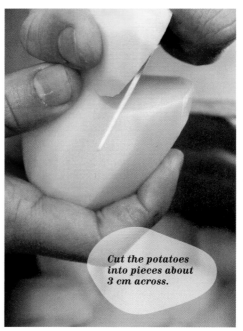

Cut the potatoes into pieces about 3 cm across.

Finely chop the garlic.

Put the flesh of the grated tomato into a sieve and leave to drain over a bowl for 15 minutes. Discard the juice.

Put a large pan over a medium heat, then pour in the oil. Add the garlic.

Continue →

As soon as the garlic starts to turn golden, add most of the chopped parsley and all of the grated tomato.

Cook for 5 minutes, then stir in the paprika.

Add the potatoes and stir until well coated in the garlic, tomato and paprika mix.

Pour in half of the stock and simmer for 20 minutes, or until the potatoes are just tender.

Season the mackerel with salt and pepper and add to the pan. Cook the fish gently for 5 minutes.

Mix the cornflour with a little cold water until smooth. Stir into the pan until the sauce thickens slightly. Stir carefully so that the potato and mackerel do not break up.

Leave to cook gently for 5 more minutes or until the fish is opaque and flakes easily away from the back bone. Meanwhile, loosen the aioli with a little of the sauce. Add to the pan.

Finish the dish by sprinkling with the remaining chopped parsley and seasoning with salt.

Serve the stew in shallow bowls.

Chocolate cookies

We do not recommend making less than the quantity given for 20 cookies. If you want to bake just a few at a time, simply cut as many slices as you need and return the dough to the freezer.

•

Five-spice is a Chinese spice mix, usually containing ground fennel, cardamom, star anise, Sichuan pepper and cinnamon. You can find it at any Chinese speciality shop.

•

If you do not have a microwave, melt the chocolate in a heatproof bowl set over a pan of barely simmering water.

	For 20 cookies	For 100 cookies
Vanilla pod	¼	1
Eggs	1	5
Sugar	80 g	400 g
Butter	2 tsp	85 g
Dark chocolate, 75% cocoa	75 g	825 g
White and dark chocolate pieces	25 g	225 g
Flour	2 tsp	85 g
Five-spice powder	½ tsp	1 tsp
Instant coffee, ground	½ tsp	1 tsp

Start →

Split the vanilla pod lengthways and scrape out the seeds with a knife.

Put the eggs into a large mixing bowl. Add the sugar.

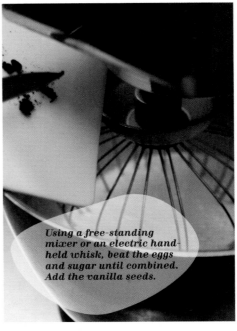

Using a free-standing mixer or an electric hand-held whisk, beat the eggs and sugar until combined. Add the vanilla seeds.

Continue to beat the egg and sugar mixture for about 5 minutes until very thick and creamy.

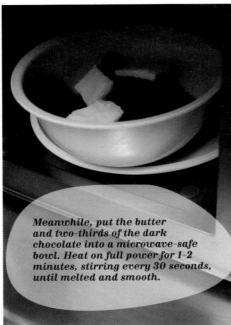

Meanwhile, put the butter and two-thirds of the dark chocolate into a microwave-safe bowl. Heat on full power for 1-2 minutes, stirring every 30 seconds, until melted and smooth.

Roughly chop the white chocolate pieces and remaining dark chocolate. Set aside.

Continue →

Pour the melted chocolate and butter into the egg and sugar mix, then beat or fold together until smooth.

Mix together the flour, five spice and coffee.

Fold into the cookie mixture.

Now fold in the chopped chocolate.

Spread the cookie dough over a large sheet of baking parchment, then roll into a cylinder about 4 cm across.

Freeze the dough until solid (about 1 hour). Unwrap, then cut the cylinder into discs 1 cm thick.

Preheat the oven to 180°C/350°F/Gas Mark 4.

Line baking trays with baking parchment, arrange the discs on the the trays and bake for 10 minutes.

Cool on a wire rack and serve.

–

Meal 3

–

Vichyssoise

–

Lamb with mustard & mint

–

Chocolate truffles

INGREDIENTS

BUY FRESH
* small red onions
* leeks
* whole lamb necks,
  cut in half
* fresh mint

IN THE CUPBOARD
* potatoes
* salt
* black peppercorns
* croutons
* extra-virgin olive oil
* olive oil
* wholegrain mustard
* soy sauce
* Worcestershire sauce
* dark chocolate,
  60% cocoa
* brandy
* cocoa powder

IN THE FRIDGE
* whole milk
* eggs
* butter
* whipping cream
  35% fat

IN THE FREEZER
* chicken stock
  (see page 57)

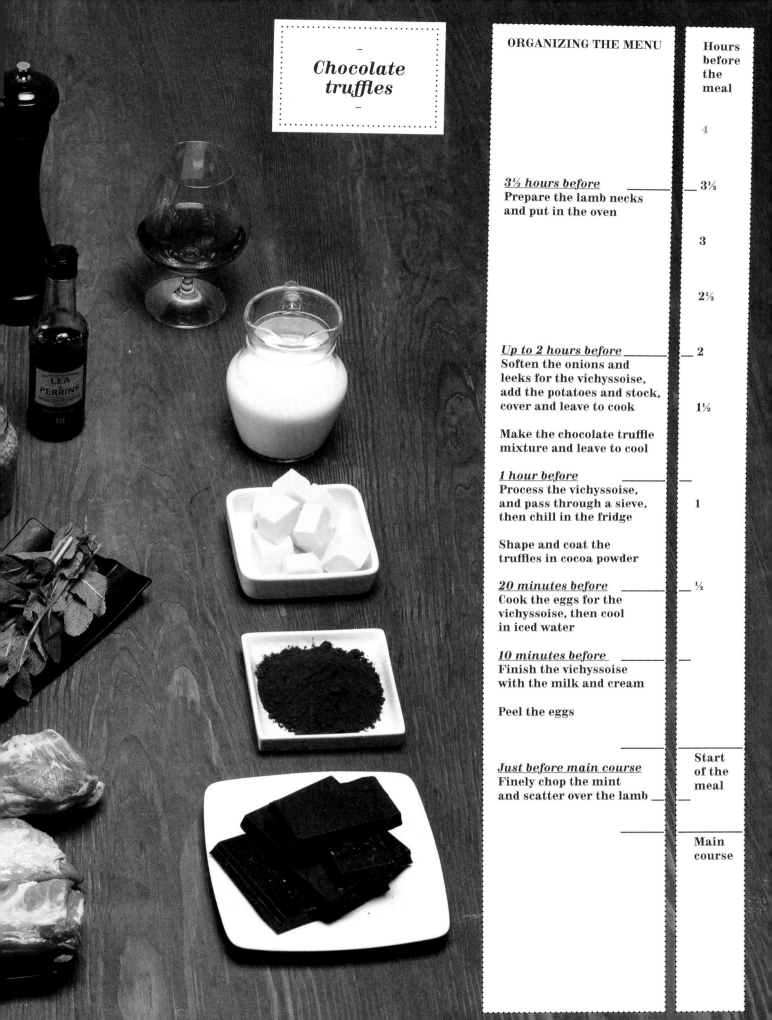

Chocolate truffles

ORGANIZING THE MENU	Hours before the meal
	4
3½ hours before **Prepare the lamb necks and put in the oven**	3½
	3
	2½
Up to 2 hours before **Soften the onions and leeks for the vichyssoise, add the potatoes and stock, cover and leave to cook**	2
	1½
Make the chocolate truffle mixture and leave to cool	
1 hour before **Process the vichyssoise, and pass through a sieve, then chill in the fridge**	1
Shape and coat the truffles in cocoa powder	
20 minutes before **Cook the eggs for the vichyssoise, then cool in iced water**	½
10 minutes before **Finish the vichyssoise with the milk and cream**	
Peel the eggs	
Just before main course **Finely chop the mint and scatter over the lamb**	Start of the meal
	Main course

Vichyssoise

Vichyssoise is a classic leek and potato soup from France.

•

We sometimes cook the eggs in a low-temperature water bath called a Roner at 63°C (145°F) for 40 minutes. This gives a soft and silky result.

•

Ready-made croutons are ideal for this recipe and will save you time. However, to make your own, see page 52.

	for 2	for 6	for 20	for 75
Potatoes	½	200 g	800 g	2.64 kg
Red onions	½	1	330 g	1 kg
Leeks	1	2	1.1 kg	3.4 kg
Butter	1½ tbsp	100 g	400 g	1.2 kg
Chicken stock (see page 57)	400 ml	1 l	2.5 l	8 l
Eggs	2	6	20	75
Whipping cream, 35% fat	40 ml	240 ml	800 ml	3 l
Croutons	2 tbsp	4 tbsp	300 g	1 kg
Extra-virgin olive oil	1 tsp	1 tbsp	50 ml	190 ml

Start →

Cut the potatoes into small pieces and drop into a bowl of cold water until needed.

Thinly slice the onion.

Trim the dark green leaves from the leeks and cut the leeks in half, lengthways. Rinse under the tap to remove any dirt or grit.

Thinly slice them.

Melt the butter in a large saucepan over a low heat, and add the onions. Cook for 5 minutes until softened but not browned.

Add the leeks and cook for another 10 minutes, stirring often, until the leeks and onions are very soft.

Meanwhile, pour the chicken stock into a large pan and bring to the boil.

Continue →

Add the potatoes to the onions and leeks.

Add the hot stock, cover and simmer for 30 minutes.

Bring a pan of water to boil. Add the eggs and boil for 3 minutes.

Cool the eggs in a bowl of iced water, then peel off the shells. Keep them in a bowl of warm water until ready to serve.

After 30 minutes of cooking, process the soup using a hand-held blender until smooth and creamy.

Pass the soup through a fine-meshed sieve and leave to cool in the pan. Chill in the fridge until very cold.

Whisk the cream into the soup, then season with salt and pepper.

Place an egg in the middle of each serving bowl, and pour in the vichyssoise.

Scatter with croutons and drizzle with the extra-virgin olive oil.

Lamb with mustard & mint

Ask your butcher to prepare the lamb necks. The excess fat should be removed, then the necks cut in half lengthways to create two large, meaty chops.

	for 2	for 6	for 20	for 75
Whole lamb necks, cut in half	1	3	10	38
Sprigs fresh mint	8	1 small bunch	2 bunches	5 bunches
Olive oil	2 tbsp	80 ml	270 ml	800 ml
Wholegrain mustard	1 tbsp	3 tbsp	270 g	800 g
Soy sauce	1 tbsp	3 tbsp	120 ml	360 ml
Worcestershire sauce	1 tbsp	3 tbsp	160 ml	480 ml
Water	1 l	1.5 l	4.3 l	16 l

Start →

Preheat the oven to 180°C/350°F/Gas Mark 4.

Pick the mint leaves from the stalks and set aside.

Season the lamb with salt and pepper.

Place a large frying pan over a high heat and add the olive oil. Brown the lamb well on each side.

Transfer to a roasting tin.

Spread the mustard over the lamb.

Continue →

Add the soy sauce, Worcestershire sauce and water.

Cover the lamb with half the mint and cover with foil.

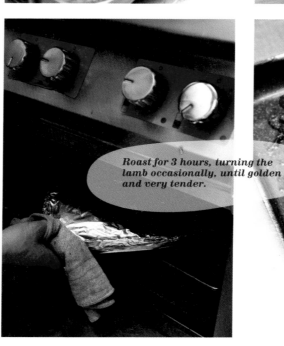

Roast for 3 hours, turning the lamb occasionally, until golden and very tender.

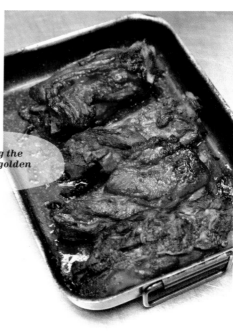

Finely chop the remaining mint leaves.

Sprinkle the chopped mint over the lamb.

Pour the sauce from the pan over the lamb and serve.

Chocolate truffles

To make chocolate hazelnut truffles, add some Nutella at the same time as the butter.

•

You can replace the brandy with another spirit or liqueur, if you like.

•

You can also pipe the truffles using a piping bag. In this case you will need to remove them from the fridge to soften before piping.

	for 2 (makes 8 truffles)	for 6	for 20	for 75
Dark chocolate, 60% cocoa	60 g	120 g	400 g	1.2 kg
Whipping cream, 35% fat	60 ml	120 ml	400 ml	1.2 ml
Butter, cut into small pieces	1 tsp	2 tsp	35 g	100 g
Brandy	½ tsp	2 tsp	18 ml	50 ml
Cocoa powder	2 tbsp	4 tbsp	50 g	100 g

Start →

Chop the chocolate into small pieces and place in a large bowl. Pour the cream into a saucepan, then bring to the boil.

Pour the hot cream over the chocolate.

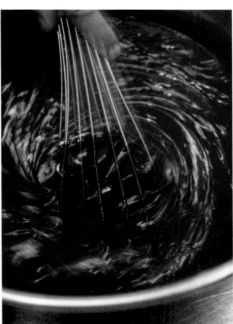

Leave the chocolate to melt for 3 minutes, then stir well with a balloon whisk, until smooth and creamy.

Continue →

Whisk in the butter.

Pour in the brandy and stir until smooth.

Cover the surface of the mixture with cling film to prevent a skin forming, then set aside to cool until firm.

Use two teaspoons to shape the mix into 15-g irregular-shaped pieces.

Drop the truffles into the cocoa powder.

Carefully roll them to coat.

Serve the truffles at room temperature.

Beans with clams

–

Salt cod & vegetable stew

–

Baked apples

–
*Beans
with
clams*
–

–
*Salt cod
& vegetable
stew*
–

INGREDIENTS

BUY FRESH
* small round clams
* long, mild red peppers
* long, mild green
  peppers
* aubergines
* courgettes
* large ripe tomatoes
* Golden Delicious
  apples
* salt cod

IN THE CUPBOARD
* tinned white beans
* salt
* black peppercorns
* onions
* garlic
* sunflower oil
* extra-virgin olive oil
* brandy
* runny honey
* ground cinnamon
* sugar

IN THE FRIDGE
* butter
* whipping cream,
  35% fat

IN THE FREEZER
* fish stock
  (see page 56)
* sofrito
  (see page 43)
* picada
  (see page 41)

Baked apples

ORGANIZING THE MENU	Hours before the meal
	4
24 hours before **Put the salt cod into a container, cover with cold water and leave in the fridge to soak**	
	3½
	3
	2½
	2
1½ hours before **Cover the clams with water and leave to soak**	1½
1 hour before **Prepare the apples and put into the oven**	1
Make the salt cod stew and leave to simmer	
25 minutes before **Cook the beans**	½
10 minutes before **Whip the cream for the apples**	
Just before eating **Add the clams to the beans**	
	Start of the meal
Just before main course **Add the salt cod to the vegetables**	
	Main course

Beans with clams

–

We use a variety of white bean known as *planchada*, which give a creamy result. Cannellini or butter beans make a good substitute.

•

If round clams are not available, use mussels or small razor clams instead.

•

The dish should be soupy. You may need to add a little more stock if you are using a wide pan. When cooking it for large numbers, add the stock before the beans so that they do not break up too much.

	for 2	for 6	for 20	for 75
Small round clams	160 g	500 g	1.6 kg	6 kg
Sofrito (see page 43)	2 tsp	2 tbsp	300 g	1 kg
Tinned white beans, drained	300 g	900 g	3 kg	10 kg
Fish stock (see page 56)	400 ml	1.5 l	3 l	7 l
Picada (see page 41)	2 tsp	2 tbsp	110 g	400 g

Start →

Pick over the clams, discarding any that are damaged.

Put the clams in a large bowl and cover with salted water.

Leave to soak for 1 hour. This will help the clams to purge themselves of any sand.

Heat the sofrito in a large pan over a medium heat.

Stir in the beans, followed by the fish stock.

Simmer the beans for 15 minutes.

Add the picada.

Lift the clams out of the water, leaving any sand behind in the bowl, and add to the pan.

Cook for 3 minutes until the clams open. Discard any clams that stay shut.

Season to taste with salt and pepper.

Serve in soup dishes.

Salt cod & vegetable stew

This traditional dish of vegetables cooked in olive oil is called *samfaina* in Catalonia.

•

You can serve the stew on toast as an open sandwich.

•

Salt cod can vary in its saltiness, so ask your fishmonger how long they would recommend to soak yours for before use. Change the water regularly.

	for 2	for 6	for 20	for 75
Onions	70 g	200 g	700 g	2.25 kg
Garlic cloves	½	2	10 g	25 g
Long, mild red peppers	50 g	150 g	500 g	2 kg
Long, mild green peppers	50 g	150 g	500 g	2 kg
Aubergine	120 g	350 g	1.2 kg	4 kg
Courgette	120 g	350 g	1.2 kg	4 kg
Ripe tomatoes	100 g	300 g	1 kg	3.5 kg
Sunflower oil	200 ml	500 ml	1 l	3 l
Extra-virgin olive oil	1½ tbsp	3 tbsp	150 ml	600 ml
Salt cod, soaked	150 g	450 g	1.5 kg	5 kg

For 2, you will need to buy 1 of each vegetable, and for 6, you will need to buy 2 of each vegetable. In both cases, choose small ones.

Start →

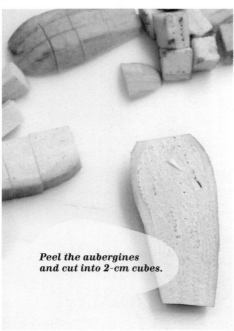

Cut the onion into 2-cm pieces.

Finely chop the garlic.

Remove the stalk, seeds and white membranes from the peppers and cut into 1.5-cm pieces.

Peel the aubergines and cut into 2-cm cubes.

Cut the courgettes to the same size.

Cut the tomatoes in half, then coarsely grate into a bowl.

Continue →

Pour the sunflower oil into a large, deep pan and place over a medium heat.

Once the oil is hot, carefully add the aubergine and courgette in small batches and fry until golden.

Drain in a colander to remove the excess oil.

Pour the olive oil into a large saucepan and place over a medium heat. Add the garlic and fry for 1 minute. Add the onion and cook for 5 minutes, until golden.

Add the peppers and cook until they start to soften.

Add the fried and drained aubergine and courgette, then add the grated tomato. Simmer for 1 hour.

When the vegetables are very soft and the tomatoes have thickened, season with salt and pepper and add enough water to give a creamy texture.

Tear the cod into pieces about 1.5 cm wide and 5 cm long. Add to the stew and simmer for 2 minutes. Do not overcook.

Remove from the heat and serve on plates, or on top of toasted bread.

Baked apples

You can use cognac, armagnac, calvados or any other similar spirit instead of the brandy.

•

You can use any type of apple, but we like Golden Delicious.

•

When preparing the dish for 2 people, you may prefer to use thick double cream instead, as it is difficult to whip small quantities of cream.

	for 2	for 6	for 20	for 75
Apples	2	6	20	75
Brandy	2 tsp	2 tbsp	120 ml	400 ml
Runny honey	2 tsp	2 tbsp	200 g	700 g
Ground cinnamon	1 pinch	2 pinches	8 g	30 g
Butter, cut into small pieces	2 tsp	2 tbsp	80 g	300 g
Whipping cream, 35% fat	60 ml	180 ml	600 ml	2 l
Sugar	½ tsp	2 tsp	80 g	300 g

Start →

Slice off the tops of the apples and reserve them.

Remove the cores using an apple corer, or cut around the cores with a small sharp knife and push them out.

Preheat the oven to 200°C/400°F/Gas Mark 6.

Cut off the bottoms of the cores and put them back into the apples. This will help to keep the filling in the apples as they bake.

Put the apples into a baking tray and drizzle with brandy.

Continue →

Pour the honey over top.

Dust the apples with cinnamon.

Put some butter inside each apple.

Top each apple with a lid and cover the tray in foil.

Bake for 1 hour, until the apples are tender.

Pour the cream into a large bowl, and add the sugar.

Whip until soft peaks form.

Lift the warm apples out from the tray and onto serving plates. Spoon over the pan juices and serve with the cream.

–

Meal 5

–

Polenta & Parmesan gratin

–

Sesame sardines with carrot salad

–

Mango with white chocolate yoghurt

INGREDIENTS

BUY FRESH
* sardines
* lemons
* carrots
* fresh mint
* mangoes

IN THE CUPBOARD
* salt
* sesame seeds
* extra-virgin olive oil
* olive oil
* Dijon mustard
* sherry vinegar
* caramelized
  hazelnuts
* quick-cook polenta
* white chocolate

IN THE FRIDGE
* Parmesan
* butter
* natural yoghurt
* whipping cream,
  35% fat

ORGANIZING THE MENU

	Hours before the meal
	4
	3½
	3
	2½
	2
	1½
1 hour before Make the white chocolate yoghurt	1
Break up the caramelized hazelnuts and set aside	½
Clean the sardines and coat in sesame seeds. Chill until needed	
Peel and slice the carrots. Make the vinaigrette	
20 minutes before Peel and cut the mango and chill	
Grate the cheese and boil the water for the polenta	
15 minutes before Make the polenta and set aside	
Just before eating Sprinkle Parmesan over the polenta and grill it	
Just before main course Fry the sardines. Dress the carrot with the vinaigrette	Start of the meal
	Main course
Just before dessert Spoon the yoghurt over the mango and sprinkle with the nuts	
	Dessert

Polenta & Parmesan gratin

–

For the creamiest polenta,
make it just before
you want to serve it.

•

Look for the quick-cook variety of
polenta, which cooks in 5–10 minutes.

	for 2	for 6	for 20	for 75
Water	300 ml	900 ml	4 l	12 l
Polenta	50 g	150 g	600 g	2 kg
Whipping cream, 35% fat	100 ml	300 ml	1.5 l	4 l
Butter	1 tsp	2 tsp	200 g	600 g
Parmesan cheese, finely grated	40 g	120 g	500 g	1.6 kg
For the gratin:				
Parmesan cheese, finely grated	1½ tbsp	4 tbsp	600 g	2 kg

Start →

Pour the water into a saucepan
and bring to the boil. Sprinkle
in the polenta a little at a time,
whisking continuously.

When all the polenta
has been added, cook
for 2 minutes over a
medium heat, whisking
continuously.

Pour in the cream and cook
for another 2 minutes.

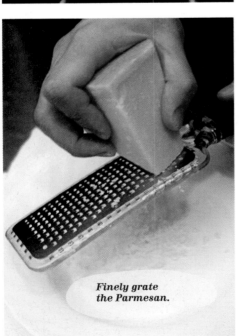

Finely grate
the Parmesan.

Gradually add the first quantity
of Parmesan cheese.

Add the butter.

Keep whisking until the polenta has thickened. Season with salt.

Pour the polenta into a large baking tray or heatproof dish. The polenta should be about 1 cm deep.

Leave the polenta to stand for 5 minutes and preheat the grill to high.

Sprinkle with the second quantity of grated Parmesan.

Grill until the cheese is golden and bubbling.

Serve immediately.

Sesame sardines with carrot salad

Ask your fishmonger to clean and gut the fish for you if you prefer.

	for 2	for 6	for 20	for 75
Medium sardines	10	30	100	375
Sesame seeds	3 tbsp	120 g	500 g	1.6 kg
Olive oil	2 tsp	2 tbsp	100 ml	300 ml
Lemons, halved	½	2	4	10
For the carrot salad:				
Carrots	2	6	2 kg	6 kg
Dijon mustard	2 tsp	2 tbsp	175 g	520 g
Sherry vinegar	2 tsp	2 tbsp	125 ml	400 ml
Extra-virgin olive oil	2 tbsp	6 tbsp	400 ml	1.2 l
Fresh mint, finely chopped	1 sprig	3 sprigs	1 bunch	2 bunches

Start →

To scale each fish, run the back of a knife firmly along the length of the body from tail to head. This is best done under a cold running tap.

Use kitchen scissors to remove the head.

Using a very sharp knife, open out the sardine from the belly side and remove the backbone.

Rinse under cold water to remove any blood.

Put the sesame seeds onto a plate. Coat the skin side of the sardines with sesame seeds.

Slice the carrots very thinly using a mandolin or vegetable peeler.

To make the vinaigrette, put the mustard in a small bowl, and whisk in the oil.

Then whisk in the sherry vinegar.

Continue →

Finely chop the mint leaves.

*Stir them into
the vinaigrette.*

*Place a non-stick frying
pan over a medium heat,
then add the oil. Season
the sardines with salt.*

*Fry on both sides
for 1 minute, or until
golden brown and juicy.*

*Transfer the sardines
to a plate, then squeeze
over the juice of the lemon.*

*Toss the carrot slices
with the vinaigrette.*

Season with salt.

*Serve the sardines
with the carrot salad.*

Mango with white chocolate yoghurt

If you prefer, toasted or caramelized almonds, walnuts or pine nuts can be substituted for the hazelnuts.

•

Take the yoghurt out of the fridge before you start, so that it is not too cold when the white chocolate is added.

	for 2	for 6	for 20	for 75
White chocolate	50 g	150 g	400 g	1.25 kg
Natural yoghurt	125 g	375 g	625 g	1.875 kg
Caramelized hazelnuts	8	24	200 g	500 g
Ripe mangoes	1	3	8	30

Start →

Break the white chocolate into cubes and put into a large heatproof bowl.

Bring a saucepan of water to a simmer, then put the bowl of chocolate over the pan. The water should not touch the bottom of the bowl.

Leave the chocolate to melt slowly, stirring regularly until smooth.

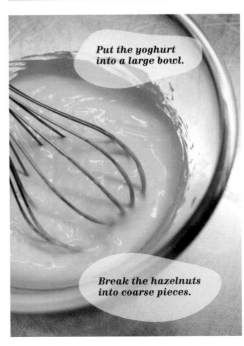

Put the yoghurt into a large bowl.

Break the hazelnuts into coarse pieces.

Gradually whisk the melted chocolate into the yoghurt to make a smooth sauce. Cool at room temperature.

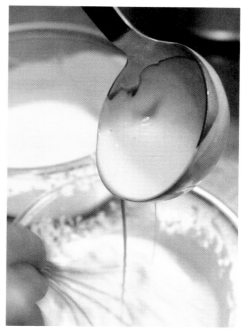

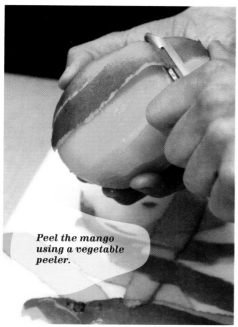

Peel the mango using a vegetable peeler.

Cut the flesh away from the fibrous stone in the middle.

Cut the mango flesh into 2-cm cubes or slices, then chill until needed.

Transfer the mango to serving plates and spoon over the yoghurt. Sprinkle with hazelnuts and serve.

Crisp omelette

–

Pork loin with peppers

–

Coconut macaroons

Crisp
omelette

INGREDIENTS

BUY FRESH
* large red peppers
* fresh parsley
* thin-cut pork loin
  steaks
* unsweetened
  desiccated coconut

IN THE CUPBOARD
* olive oil
* salted potato crisps
* garlic
* salt
* black peppercorns
* sugar

IN THE FRIDGE
* eggs

Pork loin with peppers

Coconut macaroons

Crisp omelette

It is essential to use good-quality crisps and eggs.

•

Because the crisps are salted, there is no need to season with salt.

•

For large quantities, we make large omelettes to serve 4–6 people each and place them on the table for people to help themselves.

	for 2	for 6	for 20	for 75
Olive oil	1½ tbsp	4 tbsp	100 g	200 g
Eggs	6	18	60	225
Salted potato crisps	70 g	210 g	650 g	2.25 kg

Start →

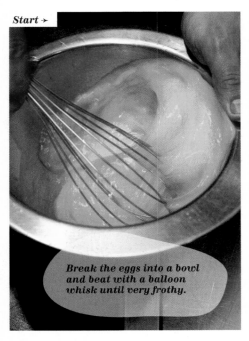

Break the eggs into a bowl and beat with a balloon whisk until very frothy.

Add the crisps, taking care not to break them, then leave to soak in the egg for for 1 minute.

Place a 25-cm non-stick frying pan over a medium heat, then add 2 teaspoons of oil.

Continue →

Pour the mixture into the pan and stir gently with a rubber spatula.

Use the spatula to loosen the omelette from the edge of the pan.

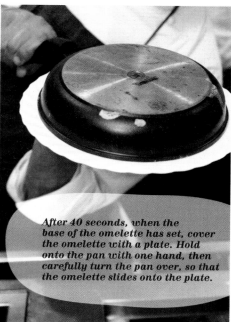

After 40 seconds, when the base of the omelette has set, cover the omelette with a plate. Hold onto the pan with one hand, then carefully turn the pan over, so that the omelette slides onto the plate.

Remove the pan and return it to the heat. Add another 2 teaspoons oil.

Slide the omelette from the plate and into the pan, so that the uncooked side is in contact with the heat. Cook for another 20 seconds.

Serve the omelette on a plate.

Pork loin with roasted peppers

This recipe also works well with beef.

	for 2	for 6	for 20	for 75
Large red peppers	1	2	8	30
Olive oil, plus extra for frying	3½ tbsp	100 ml	150 ml	425 ml
Garlic cloves	1	3	80 g	225 g
Sprigs fresh parsley	1	3	½ bunch	1 bunch
Thin-cut pork loin steaks	6	18	60	225

Start →

Preheat the oven to 200°C/400°F/Gas Mark 6. Rinse the peppers, then place in a roasting tin while still slightly wet.

Drizzle with a little oil and roast for 45 minutes.

Fill a small saucepan with water, then add the garlic. Bring the pan to the boil.

Lift the garlic out of the water and into a bowl of iced water to quickly cool. Repeat this twice, starting with cold water in the saucepan each time.

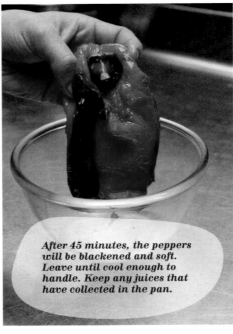

After 45 minutes, the peppers will be blackened and soft. Leave until cool enough to handle. Keep any juices that have collected in the pan.

Peel the skin from the peppers and remove the seeds. Do this over a bowl to catch any juices.

Continue →

Cut the flesh into thin strips.

Put the peppers and the reserved juices into a pan and simmer over a low heat for 5 minutes.

Pick the leaves from the parsley stems.

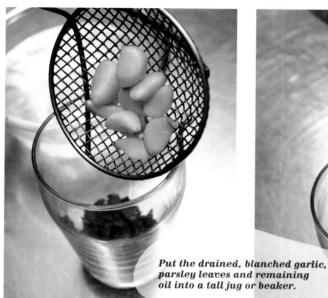

Put the drained, blanched garlic, parsley leaves and remaining oil into a tall jug or beaker.

Process with a hand-held blender until finely chopped.

Place a large frying pan over a high heat and add a little olive oil. Fry the pork for 1½ minutes, until golden on both sides and juicy in the middle.

Season the pork with salt and pepper, and serve with the peppers. Finish with a tablespoon of the garlic and parsley oil.

Coconut macaroons

We do not recommend making less than the amount given for 15 macaroons, to ensure a good result. Any leftover macaroons will keep for a few days in an airtight container.

	for 2 (makes 15)	for 6 (makes 30)	for 20	for 75
Unsweetened desiccated coconut	100 g	200 g	600 g	1.5 kg
Sugar	100 g	200 g	600 g	1.5 kg
Eggs	1	2	5	15

Start →

Preheat the oven to 180°C/350°F/Gas Mark 4 and line a large baking sheet with baking parchment. Mix the coconut and sugar in a large bowl.

Beat the eggs with a balloon whisk.

Stir the eggs into the coconut and sugar.

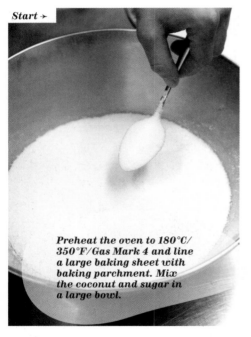

Mix with your hands until even.

Continue →

Using your hands or two teaspoons, shape the mix into walnut-size balls, about 15 g each.

Place on a baking tray.

Bake for 13 minutes, or until slightly golden.

Leave to cool before serving.

Saffron risotto with mushrooms

–

Catalan-style turkey

–

Yoghurt foam with strawberries

INGREDIENTS

BUY FRESH
* white mushrooms
* lemons
* red onions
* turkey drumsticks
* strawberries

IN THE CUPBOARD
* saffron
* olive oil
* onions
* white wine
* risotto rice
* salt
* black peppercorns
* raisins
* prunes
* *vino rancio* or dry
  sherry
* tinned chopped
  tomatoes
* pine nuts
* sugar, optional
* N$_2$O cartridges
  for the siphon

IN THE FRIDGE
* butter
* Parmesan cheese
* natural yoghurt
* whipping cream
  35% fat

IN THE FREEZER
* chicken stock
  (see page 57)

(see page 57)

–
Saffron risotto
with
mushrooms
–

Catalan-style turkey

Yoghurt foam with strawberries

ORGANIZING THE MENU

**24 hours before**
Soak the raisins and
prunes in the _vino rancio_

**1½ hours before**
Start the turkey. Simmer
for 30 minutes then cover
and keep warm

Make the yoghurt foam,
then chill in the fridge

Chop the onions
for the risotto

**40 minutes before**
Heat the chicken stock
and toast the saffron
for the risotto

**30 minutes before**
Start cooking the risotto

Fry the pine nuts, ready
to finish the turkey

Wash and halve the
strawberries

**5 minutes before**
Slice the mushrooms

Finish the risotto with
the butter and cheese and
top with the mushrooms

Sprinkle the turkey
with pine nuts

**Just before dessert**
Dispense the yoghurt foam
into bowls, then finish
with the strawberries

Hours before the meal
4
3½
3
2½
2
1½
1
½
Start of the meal
Dessert

Saffron risotto with mushrooms

It is essential to choose the right rice for your risotto. Rice varieties such as arborio, carnaroli and vialone nano are commonly used in Italy. If these varieties are not available, you will need to use a round-grained rice with a high starch content.

	for 2	for 6	for 20	for 75
Chicken stock (see page 57)	600 ml	1.8 l	7 l	22 l
Saffron strands	1 pinch	2 pinches	1.2 g	4 g
Olive oil	1½ tbsp	50 ml	125 ml	425 ml
Onion, finely chopped	1 tsp	2 tsp	120 g	400 g
White wine	2 tbsp	4 tbsp	200 ml	750 ml
Risotto rice	180 g	540 g	1.8 kg	7 kg
Medium white mushrooms	2	6	800 g	3 kg
Butter	1 tsp	1 tbsp	60 g	200 g
Parmesan cheese, finely grated	30 g	100 g	300 g	1 kg
Lemon juice	1 tsp	2 tsp	35 ml	120 ml

Start →

Pour the stock into a saucepan. Cover with a lid and bring to a simmer.

Wrap the saffron threads in aluminium foil.

Toast in a frying pan for 1 minute over a medium heat, taking care not to let it burn. Cool.

Heat the oil in a large pan over a medium heat. Add the onion and fry for about 5 minutes until softened but not browned.

Pour in the white wine and scrape up any sediment from the bottom of the pan.

When most of the wine has boiled away, add the rice and stir for 3 minutes.

Add a ladle of hot stock. Stir the rice frequently for 2–3 minutes to prevent sticking.

Pour in the remaining stock. Chop the toasted saffron and sprinkle into the pan.

Cook the rice for 16 more minutes, stirring frequently.

Meanwhile, quickly wash and drain the mushrooms. Dry with kitchen paper, then finely slice using a mandolin or sharp knife.

When the rice has absorbed most of the liquid and is just firm to the bite, add the butter.

Add the Parmesan cheese. Stir well until the rice becomes creamy. Season with salt, pepper and lemon juice. Spoon the risotto onto serving plates.

Scatter the mushroom slices over the risotto. The heat from the rice will lightly 'cook' the mushrooms.

Catalan-style turkey

Vino rancio is a Catalan fortified oxidized wine. If you cannot find it, use dry sherry instead.

	for 2	for 6	for 20	for 75
Raisins	30 g	90 g	300 g	1 kg
Pitted prunes	40 g	120 g	400 g	1.5 kg
Vino rancio	6 tbsp	250 ml	800 ml	3 l
Red onions, thinly sliced	200 g	600 g	2.4 kg	8 kg
Turkey drumsticks	2	6	20	75
Olive oil	1½ tbsp	3 tbsp	150 ml	400 ml
Tomatoes, chopped	100 g	250 g	1.2 kg	5 kg
Water	240 ml	720 ml	2.4 l	8 l
Pine nuts	2 tsp	2 tbsp	100 g	300 g

For 2 people you will need 1 onion, and for 6 people you will need 3.

Start →

Put the raisins and prunes in a bowl and pour over the vino rancio.

Leave to soak for 12 hours.

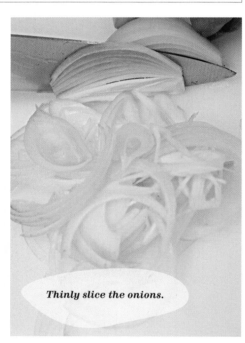

Thinly slice the onions.

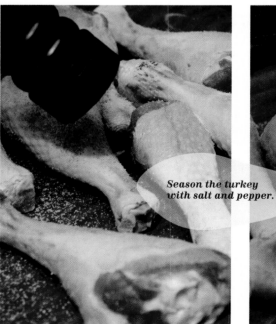

Season the turkey with salt and pepper.

Put a wide pan over a medium heat, then add most of the oil. Brown the turkey for 10 minutes until golden all over.

Continue →

Add the onions.

Fry the onions and turkey for about 10 minutes, stirring often, until the onions are caramelized and dark golden brown.

Drain the vino rancio from the fruit, then add to the pan.

When most of the vino rancio has evaporated, add the chopped tomato and continue to cook until everything is well caramelized.

Pour in the water, turn the heat down and simmer for 30 minutes.

Add the raisins and prunes. Cover the pan and leave to cook for another hour, or until the turkey is very tender and the sauce is thick and tasty.

Meanwhile, heat the remaining oil in a frying pan, then add the pine nuts. Cook over a low heat for about 5 minutes, stirring often, until golden.

Put the turkey onto a serving dish, cover with the sauce, raisins and prunes. Finish by sprinkling with pine nuts.

Yoghurt foam with strawberries

–

If you prefer a sweeter dessert,
add 2 tsp sugar for every 375 g yoghurt.

•

You can substitute any seasonal fruit
for the strawberries, such as peach,
apricot, banana or pineapple.

•

Look for small strawberries that weigh
around 15 g each. Allow 3 per person.

	for 2	for 4–6	for 20	for 75
Natural yoghurt	-	375 g	1 kg	3.5 kg
Whipping cream, 35% fat	-	100 ml	250 ml	900 ml
N₂O cartridges for the siphon	-	1	6	12
Strawberries	-	180–270 g	900 g	3.4 kg

The minimum quantity of foam
you can make in a siphon is 4–6 portions.
If you do not have a siphon, you can whip
the cream and yogurt with a whisk,
although the texture will not be as airy.

Use a 0.5-litre siphon for 4–6 people,
2 x 2-litre siphons for 20, and 6 x 1-litre
siphons for 75.

Start →

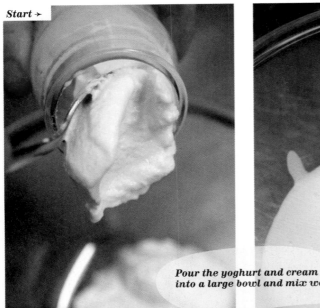

Pour the yoghurt and cream
into a large bowl and mix well.

Sweeten with sugar,
if you like.

Pass the mixture through a fine-
meshed sieve, into the siphon.

Continue →

Charge the siphon with the cartridge. Leave to cool in the fridge.

Wash and hull the strawberries, then halve them.

Shake the siphon vigorously just before serving.

Dispense the foam into small bowls or glasses, then top with the strawberries.

Roasted aubergine with miso dressing

–

Sausages with tomato sauce

–

Crème Catalane

Roasted aubergine with miso dressing

Sausages with tomato sauce

INGREDIENTS

BUY FRESH
* aubergines
* pork sausages
* fresh thyme
* lemons
* oranges

IN THE CUPBOARD
* sesame seeds
* dashi powder
* red miso paste
* soy sauce
* toasted sesame oil
* sunflower oil
* olive oil
* garlic
* *vino rancio*
  or dry sherry
* cinnamon sticks
* green anise, star anise
  or fennel seeds
* vanilla pods
* sugar
* cornflour

IN THE FRIDGE
* whipping cream,
  35% fat
* whole milk
* eggs

IN THE FREEZER
* tomato sauce
  (see page 42)

ORGANIZING THE MENU

	Hours before the meal
	4
	3½
3 hours before Make the Crème Catalane and leave to cool	3
	2½
2 hours before Bake the aubergines and leave to cool	2
	1½
One hour before Blend the miso dressing	1
Peel and slice the aubergines	½
15 minutes before Dress the aubergines with miso	
Cook the sausages and serve	
5 minutes before Finish the aubergines with the sesame seeds	
Reheat the tomato sauce ready to serve with the sausages	
	Start of the meal
Just before dessert Blowtorch the sugar on the Crème Catalane	
	Dessert

Roasted aubergine with miso dressing

Dashi is a traditional Japanese stock made with kombu seaweed and *katsuobushi* (dried bonito or tuna), and adds a unique savouriness to soups, dressings and other dishes.

•

Also important in Japanese cuisine, miso is a paste made from fermented soya beans. Both ingredients can be bought from Asian food shops and some larger supermarkets.

•

The miso dressing also goes well with other roasted vegetables, such as courgettes or potatoes.

	for 2	for 6	for 20	for 75
Medium-sized aubergines	2	6	20	75
Sesame seeds	2 tbsp	6 tbsp	150 g	500 g
Water	50 ml	150 ml	500 ml	1.6 l
Dashi powder	2 tsp	2 tbsp	50 g	160 g
Red miso paste	½ tsp	1 tbsp	40 g	150 g
Soy sauce	2 tsp	2 tbsp	60 ml	200 ml
Toasted sesame oil	1 tsp	1 tbsp	30 ml	100 ml
Sunflower oil	2 tbsp	6 tbsp	150 ml	500 ml

Start →

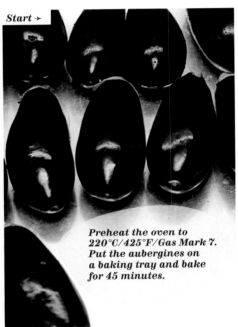

Preheat the oven to 220°C/425°F/Gas Mark 7. Put the aubergines on a baking tray and bake for 45 minutes.

Put the sesame seeds in a frying pan and heat gently for 5 minutes, stirring often, until golden.

For the miso dressing, put the water into a tall jug or jar.

Add the dashi powder, miso paste, soy sauce, sesame oil and sunflower oil.

Process with a hand-held blender until slightly thickened.

Continue →

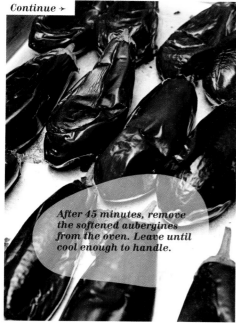

After 45 minutes, remove the softened aubergines from the oven. Leave until cool enough to handle.

Peel the skins off the aubergines.

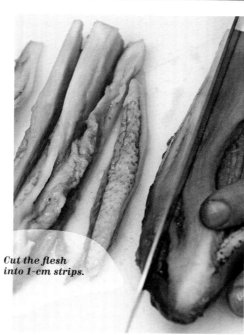

Cut the flesh into 1-cm strips.

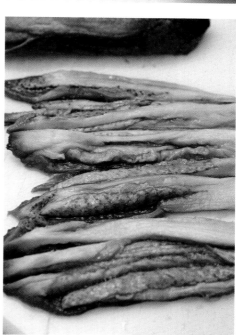

Process the miso dressing again to make sure it has not separated. Arrange the aubergines in a serving dish and spoon over the dressing.

Let the aubergines cool completely, then sprinkle with the sesame seeds and serve.

Sausages with tomato sauce

If you wish, use shop-bought tomato sauce, flavoured with a little extra-virgin olive oil (1 tsp per 150 g).

•

Vino rancio is a Catalan fortified oxidized wine. If you cannot find it, use dry sherry instead.

•

You could serve the sausages with simple roast vegetables such as potatoes or courgettes.

	for 2	for 6	for 20	for 75
Olive oil	3 tbsp	9 tbsp	150 ml	500 ml
Pork sausages	150 g	900 g	3 kg	11 kg
Garlic cloves	2	6	40 g	120 g
Sprigs fresh thyme	1	2	6 g	20 g
Vino rancio or dry sherry	2 tbsp	100 ml	350 ml	1.3 l
Tomato sauce (see page 42)	150 g	450 g	1.5 kg	5 kg

Start →

Heat the oil in a large frying pan.

Add the sausages and cook for 5 minutes, or until golden underneath.

Tuck the whole garlic cloves and thyme between the sausages.

Turn the sausages over.

When the sausages are well browned and cooked through, remove the pan from the heat.

Add the vino rancio and loosen any sediment from the bottom of the pan with a wooden spoon.

Heat the tomato sauce in a saucepan.

Put the sausages in a serving dish.

Spoon over some of the cooking juices and garlic.

Pour the tomato sauce over the sausages to serve.

Crème Catalane

Crème Catalane (or Crema Catalana), is one of the oldest desserts in Europe and appears in medieval Catalan literature.

•

Instead of caramelizing the surface of the crème with a blowtorch, you can scatter it with crushed pieces of dark caramel.

•

We do not recommend making a smaller quantity than given for 4 people. The crème can be set in individual ramekins and stored in the fridge for a few days.

	for 2	for 4	for 20	for 75
Whole milk	-	250 ml	1.2 l	4 l
Whipping cream, 35% fat	-	4 tbsp	300 ml	1 l
Cinnamon sticks	-	¼	2	4
Lemon zest	-	1 strip	2 strips	4 strips
Orange zest	-	1 strip	2 strips	4 strips
Green anise, star anise or fennel seeds	-	1 pinch	3 g	10 g
Vanilla pods, split	-	½	1½	4
Egg yolks	-	3	250 g	850 g
Sugar	-	45 g	225 g	750 g
Cornflour	-	2 tsp	50 g	180 g

Start →

Pour the milk and cream into a large saucepan.

Add the cinnamon, strips of lemon and orange zest, anise or fennel seeds and vanilla pods.

Bring the milk and cream mixture to the boil over a gentle heat.

Put the egg yolks, sugar and cornflour into a large bowl.

Whisk until smooth.

Strain the hot milk and cream into the egg yolk mixture, whisking continuously.

Return to a clean pan, then cook over a medium heat, whisking continuously, for 10 minutes.

When the mix is thickened and smooth, ladle into a heatproof dish and leave to cool.

Cover the top of the crème with an even layer of sugar.

Use a blowtorch to caramelize the sugar. Let the sugar set hard before serving.

Lime-marinated fish

—

Ossobuco

—

Piña colada

INGREDIENTS

BUY FRESH
* fresh meagre or sea
  bass fillet
* limes
* small green onions
* fresh coriander
* veal shin
* carrots
* celery
* fresh parsley
* lemons
* oranges
* pineapples

IN THE CUPBOARD
* garlic
* onions
* olive oil
* salt
* black peppercorns
* flour
* white wine
* bay leaves
* coconut milk
* white rum

IN THE FRIDGE
* butter

IN THE FREEZER
* tomato sauce
  (see page 42)
* beef stock
  (see page 58)

Piña colada

ORGANIZING THE MENU		Hours before the meal
		4
		3½
		3
2½ hours before Make the ossobuco and leave to cook in the oven		2½
2 hours before Make the piña colada mix and chill		2
		1½
		1
30 minutes before Slice the fish and chill until needed. Slice the onions and prepare the dressing		½
Make the gremolata		
Just before eating Season the fish and finish with the onion, dressing and coriander		
		Start of the meal
Just before main course Sprinkle the gremolata over the ossobuco		
		Main course
Just before dessert Pour the piña colada into small glasses or bowls with your choice of topping		
		Dessert

Lime-marinated fish

This dish is a *tiradito*, a Peruvian dish similar to ceviche, which consists of thinly sliced fish with lime juice.

•

We make this dish with meagre, a large, white fish with firm flesh popular in Spain and the Mediterranean. If you cannot find meagre, use another white fish such as sea bass.

•

Ask your fishmonger to remove the skin and any bones from the fish, or refer to the instructions for skinning salmon on page 352.

	for 2	for 6	for 20	for 75
Fresh fish fillet	150 g	500 g	2 kg	8 kg
Lime juice	1 tbsp	85 ml	210 ml	660 ml
Small green onions (or use the white parts from a bunch of spring onions)	½	1	300 g	900 g
Sprigs fresh coriander	4	12	1 bunch	3 bunches
Olive oil	4 tbsp	150 ml	500 ml	1.8 l

Start →

Cut the fish into thin slices.

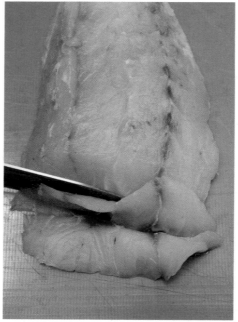

Arrange on a serving dish, without overlapping too much. Chill in the fridge.

Squeeze the limes, then pass the juice through a fine-meshed sieve.

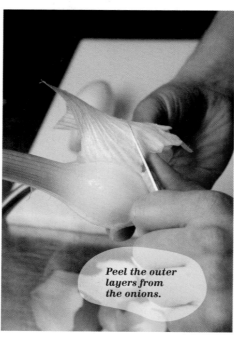

Peel the outer layers from the onions.

Thinly slice them.

Continue →

Pick the coriander leaves from the stems and chop finely.

Slowly pour the oil into the lime juice, whisking continuously with a balloon whisk (or using a hand-held blender) to make a slightly thickened and cloudy dressing.

Mix the onions with the lime juice and oil.

Scatter with the green onion and season with salt.

Pour the dressing over the fish and sprinkle with the chopped coriander.

Ossobuco

The word *ossobuco* is Italian
for 'bone with a hole', and refers
to the cut of veal used in this famous
dish. The meat surrounds a thick piece
of bone, which is full of marrow.
The marrow enriches the sauce
and should be eaten as part of the dish.

•

The gremolata (a mixture of chopped
parsley and garlic with orange and
lemon zest) is sprinkled over just before
serving, so that the fresh citrus oils in
the skin are still fragrant.

	for 2	for 6	for 20	for 75
Carrots, chopped	1 tsp	1½ tbsp	150 g	400 g
Celery, chopped	1 tsp	2 tbsp	175 g	520 g
Onions, chopped	1	2	1 kg	3 kg
Garlic cloves, finely chopped	1	3	50 g	150 g
Veal shin pieces, 250 g each	2	6	20	75
Flour	1½ tbsp	4 tbsp	150 g	400 g
Butter	1½ tbsp	100 g	450 g	1.4 kg
White wine	6 tbsp	240 ml	1.1 l	3.2 l
Dried bay leaves	2	4	15 g	40 g
Tomato sauce (see page 42)	2 tsp	2 tbsp	330 g	1 kg
Beef stock (see page 58)	500 ml	1.5 l	8 l	24 l
For the gremolata:				
Fresh parsley, finely chopped	2 tsp	2 tbsp	½ bunch	1 bunch
Garlic cloves, finely chopped	1	3	20 g	50 g
Lemons	1	2	3	5
Oranges	1	2	3	5

Start →

Cut the carrots into sticks
about 5 mm across, then
cut into 5-mm cubes.

Repeat with the celery.

Roughly chop the onion.

Continue →

Finely chop the garlic.

Season the veal shins with salt and pepper.

Dust the meat with the flour.

Pat away any excess flour.

Put a large pan over a high heat, then add the butter.

When the butter foams, add the shins.

Brown the shins on both sides, then remove from the pan.

Turn the heat to medium, then add the carrot and the rest of the butter to the pan. Stir for 1 minute.

Continue →

Continue →

Add the onion, celery and garlic, then cook gently for 10 minutes, stirring often, until the vegetables have softened.

Pour in the white wine and loosen any sediment from the bottom of the pan with a wooden spoon.

Preheat the oven to 200°C/ 400°F/Gas Mark 6.

When the wine has almost evaporated, add the bay leaves and tomato sauce. Cook over a medium heat for 10 more minutes until thickened.

Put the browned veal shins into a roasting tin. Spoon over the vegetables, then pour in the beef stock or water.

Cover the pan with foil and cook in the oven for 2 hours, until the meat is very tender.

Meanwhile, prepare the gremolata. Finely chop the parsley and garlic, then mix in small bowl. Finely grate in the zest of the lemon and orange, then mix well.

Sprinkle the gremolata over the ossobuco just before serving.

Piña colada

We like to serve this topped with more chopped pineapple, crushed meringues, freeze-dried fruit or nuts.

•

To choose a ripe pineapple, look for one in which the central leaves can be pulled out easily.

	for 2	for 6	for 20	for 75
Pineapples	½	1	5 (3.5 kg)	18 (13 kg)
Coconut milk	3 tbsp	100 g	350 g	2.8 kg
White rum	1½ tbsp	65 ml	225 ml	1.6 l

Start →

Remove the top and bottom from the pineapple. Cut away the skin and the first 5 mm of flesh.

Slice the pineapple in half lengthways, then cut into chunks.

Put into a deep container, then process with a hand-held blender until smooth. Alternatively, use a food processor.

Add the coconut milk and rum, then blend again.

Strain the mixture through a fine-meshed sieve, then chill in the fridge.

Serve the piña colada in bowls or glasses, with your choice of topping.

Miso soup with clams

–

Mackerel with vinaigrette

–

Almond biscuits

INGREDIENTS

BUY FRESH
* small round clams
* silken tofu
* fresh mackerel
* ripe tomatoes
* fresh basil
* fresh thyme
* black olive paste

IN THE CUPBOARD
* dashi powder
* red miso paste
* small dried chillies
* extra-virgin olive oil
* pickled capers
* salt
* black pepper
* sugar
* ground almonds
* whole toasted
  Marcona almonds

IN THE FRIDGE
* eggs

IN THE FREEZER
* ice cream

Almond
biscuits

ORGANIZING THE MENU

	Hours before the meal
	4
	3½
	3
	2½
	2
	1½
1 hour before Soak the clams in salted water	1
Make and bake the almond biscuits	½
Prepare all the ingredients for the fish	
15 minutes before Make the miso soup base and cut the tofu into cubes	
5 minutes before Add the clams to the soup. Blend the soup and remaining tofu	
	Start of the meal
Just before main course Fry the fish	
Take the ice cream out of the freezer so that it is soft enough to scoop	
	Main course

Miso soup with clams

Before cooking, pick over the clams, discarding any that are damaged. Put the clams into a large bowl, cover with salted cold water and leave for 1 hour. This will help the clams to purge themselves of any sand.

•

You could also use other types of clam or mussels, increasing the cooking time if they are larger.

	for 2	for 6	for 20	for 75
Water	425 ml	1.3 l	4.5 l	14 l
Dashi powder	½ tsp	2 tsp	30 g	100 g
Red miso paste	2 tsp	100 g	400 g	1.2 kg
Silken tofu	150 g	450 g	1 kg	7 kg
Small round clams	120 g	400 g	1.5 kg	5 kg

Start →

Pour the water into a large pan and add the dashi powder and red miso paste.

Process with a hand-held blender until well mixed.

Cut the tofu into 2-cm cubes.

Place tofu into serving bowls, allowing 5 per person.

Continue →

Rinse the clams under cold water.

Bring the soup to the boil, then add the clams.

Cook for 3 minutes or until the clams open. Remove from the heat.

Lift the clams out of the soup with a slotted spoon.

Place the clams on top of the tofu in the serving bowls, discarding any that have not opened.

Add the remaining tofu to the soup and blend until creamy and smooth.

Ladle the soup over the clams and tofu and serve.

Mackerel with vinaigrette

Ask your fishmonger to clean, gut and prepare the fish if you prefer.

•

Other types of small whole fish, such as sardines, can be used instead.

	for 2	for 6	for 20	for 75
Mackerel, 200 g each	2	6	20	75
Ripe tomatoes	1	3	750 g	2 kg
Small dried chillies	1	3	15	40
Extra-virgin olive oil	120 ml, plus 2 tsp	200 ml, plus 1½ tbsp	1 l, plus 100 ml	3.2 l, plus 200 ml
Pickled capers	2 tsp	2 tbsp	100 g	300 g
Sprigs fresh thyme	2	6	20	80
Black olive paste	1 tsp	2 tsp	60 g	190 g
Fresh basil	1 sprigs	3 sprigs	1 bunch	2 bunches

Start →

Cut the fins from the fish with kitchen scissors. Cut out the gills.

Slit the fish down the middle, leaving two halves joined by the head. Snip out the backbone with scissors.

Cut a small cross into the bottom of each tomato, then blanch them in a pan of boiling water for 30 seconds.

Plunge into a bowl of iced water.

Skin the tomatoes.

Cut in half, scoop out the seeds and cut into 5-mm cubes.

Continue →

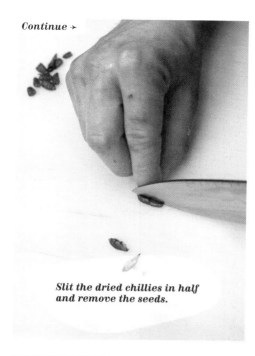

Slit the dried chillies in half and remove the seeds.

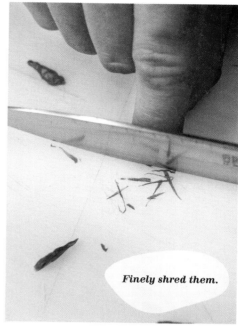

Finely shred them.

Put the diced tomato into a bowl, add the first quantity of olive oil, the shredded chilli, capers and thyme sprigs.

Season with salt and pepper.

Loosen the black olive paste with most of the remaining olive oil.

Place a large frying pan over a medium heat, add a little oil and put the fish in the pan skin-side down. Fry the fish for 3 minutes, or until golden underneath.

Cook on the second side for 3 minutes, then lift the fish onto a serving plate, flesh facing upwards. It should be golden and juicy.

Pick the smallest leaves from the basil sprigs. Spoon the tomato vinaigrette over the fish, scatter with the basil leaves then add a few spots of black olive paste.

Almond biscuits

We do not recommend making any less than the quantity given for 12 biscuits. Any leftover biscuits will keep in an airtight container for several days.

•

The biscuits can be served with any flavour of ice cream, but we like to serve them with nougat ice cream.

•

Marcona almonds are a sweet-flavoured variety from Spain. Any good-quality almonds can be substituted.

	for 2	for 6 (makes 12 almond biscuits)	for 20	for 75
Egg whites	-	1	95 g	280 g
Sugar	-	135 g	315 g	945 g
Ground almonds	-	135 g	315 g	945 g
Whole toasted Marcona almonds	-	12	150 g	500 g
Ice cream	-	300 g	2 kg	5 kg

Start →

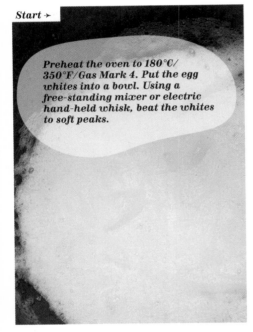

Preheat the oven to 180°C/350°F/Gas Mark 4. Put the egg whites into a bowl. Using a free-standing mixer or electric hand-held whisk, beat the whites to soft peaks.

Add the sugar.

Whisk the whites again until stiff and glossy.

Add the ground almonds, then use a rubber spatula to fold them carefully into the meringue until evenly combined.

Try to preserve as much of the air in the meringue as possible.

166

Continue →

Line a baking sheet with parchment paper. Scoop tablespoons of the mixture onto the tray, spacing them well apart.

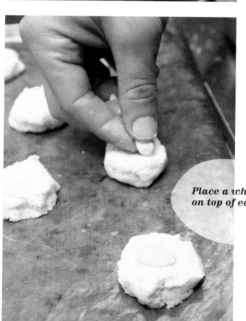

Place a whole almond on top of each mound.

Bake in the oven for 14 minutes, or until pale golden and slightly cracked.

Cool on the baking sheet, then transfer to a rack to cool completely.

Serve alone or with ice cream.

Fried eggs with asparagus

–

Chicken wings with mushrooms

–

Sangria with fruit

INGREDIENTS

BUY FRESH
* thin asparagus spears
* chicken wings
* mushrooms
* fresh thyme
* pink grapefruit
* oranges
* lemons
* apples
* pears
* peaches
* fresh mint

IN THE CUPBOARD
* olive oil
* salt
* black peppercorns
* garlic
* dried bay leaves
* white wine
* red wine
* sugar
* Cointreau
* ground cinnamon

IN THE FRIDGE
* eggs

170

ORGANIZING THE MENU	Hours before the meal
	4
	3½
	3
	2½
	2
	1½
1¼ hours before Make the sangria and chill in the fridge	1
40 minutes before Brown the chicken wings	½
Trim the asparagus	
Prepare the fruit for the sangria and chill in the fridge	
10 minutes before Heat the oil for the eggs and cook the asparagus	
Finish cooking the chicken wings	
Just before eating Fry the eggs and serve with the asparagus	
	Start of the meal
Just before dessert Put the fruit into serving bowls, pour in the sangria and finish with mint leaves	
	Dessert

Fried eggs with asparagus

You can replace the asparagus with shavings of cured ham, sautéed mushrooms or Padrón peppers, if you like.

•

The oil used for frying the eggs can be strained and used to fry other things, such as peppers.

•

When preparing for large numbers, we like to break the eggs into individual cups before we start cooking.

	for 2	for 6	for 20	for 75
Thin asparagus spears	14	42	140	525
Olive oil	200 ml	500 ml	2 l	5 l
Eggs	4	12	40	150

Start →

Hold an asparagus spear towards the stalk end, then bend it. The spear will snap, leaving you with a tough piece and tender a tip about 12 cm long.

Alternatively, slice the tough ends off with a knife.

In preparation for cooking the eggs, pour most of the olive oil into a deep frying pan and place over a medium heat.

While the oil heats up, put another frying pan over a high heat. Add a small amount of the remaining oil and add the asparagus tips.

Fry the asparagus for 3-4 minutes, turning regularly, until just tender. Transfer to a serving plate and keep warm.

Continue →

Break the eggs into cups, then carefully slide them one at a time into the hot oil.

Fry the eggs for 1½ minutes, until the whites are crisp at the edges but the yolks are still soft.

Lift the eggs from the oil using a slotted spoon. Drain well, then place on top of the asparagus. Season with salt before serving.

The eggs can also be served with sautéed mushrooms (left) or Padrón peppers (right) instead of asparagus.

Chicken wings with mushrooms

Farmed mushrooms, such as white mushrooms, king trumpet and shimeji (pictured) are ideal for this recipe, and available all year round. Wild mushrooms such as chanterelles are reasonably priced when in season, and would make the dish even better.

	for 2	for 6	for 20	for 75
Chicken wings	6	18	60	225
Olive oil	4 tbsp	100 ml	900 ml	2.1 l
Mushrooms	120 g	360 g	1.2 kg	4.5 kg
Garlic cloves	10	30	400 g	1.4 kg
Dried bay leaves	1	3	14	38
Fresh thyme sprigs	1	3	10	30
White wine	4 tbsp	180 ml	950 ml	2.25 l
Water	50 ml	150 ml	300 ml	1 l

Start →

Use strong kitchen scissors or poultry shears to remove the tips of the chicken wings, then cut each wing in half through the joint.

Season the wings with salt and pepper.

Heat the oil in a large pan and add the wings.

Cook them gently for 30 minutes, turning regularly, until well browned.

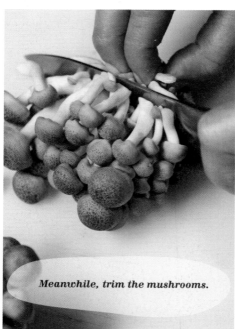

Meanwhile, trim the mushrooms.

Slice any that are large.

Roughly slice the garlic.

Add the garlic to the chicken and cook for 5 more minutes.

Add the bay leaves and thyme.

Pour in the white wine.

Turn up the heat and cook until the wine has reduced a little.

Add the mushrooms and cook for 2 minutes, stirring.

Pour in the water, then leave to simmer for 5 minutes until the mushrooms are just tender.

Serve the chicken wings and mushrooms together.

Sangria with fruit

We like to use Granny Smith apples and Blanquilla pears, but you could use other varieties.

	for 2	for 6	for 20	for 75
Orange juice, freshly squeezed	2 tbsp	6 tbsp	900 ml	2.4 l
Red wine	4 tbsp	1.8 l	800 ml	2 l
Sugar	2 tsp	2 tbsp	200 g	680 g
Cointreau	2 tsp	1½ tbsp	125 ml	375 ml
Ground cinnamon	1 pinch	2 pinches	2 g	7 g
Lemons	½	1	2	5
Pink grapefruit	½	1	5	15
Oranges	½	1	5	15
Apples	½	1	5	15
Pears	½	1	5	15
Peaches	½	1	5	15
Fresh mint	4 leaves	12 leaves	½ bunch	1 bunch

Start →

Squeeze the oranges.

Strain the juice through a fine-meshed sieve.

Add the red wine.

Add the sugar.

Finally, add the Cointreau.

Continue →

Stir in the cinnamon.

Finely grate in the lemon zest. Leave to infuse while you prepare the fruit.

Cut the top and bottom from the grapefruit and oranges, then remove the pith and skin.

Remove the flesh from each segment, holding the fruit over a small bowl to catch any juices.

Peel and core the apples and cut into 1.5-cm wedges.

Peel and core the pears and cut into 1.5-cm wedges.

Peel and halve the peach, remove the stone, then cut the flesh into 1.5-cm wedges.

Add the fruit to the sangria and leave to marinate for 1 hour.

Scoop out the fruit and place in a bowl with a few mint leaves. Pour the sangria on top.

Potato salad

–

Thai beef curry

–

Strawberries in vinegar

Potato
salad

INGREDIENTS

BUY FRESH
* large new potatoes
* fresh chives
* small green onions
* frankfurters
* blade of beef
* fresh root ginger
* fresh coriander
* medium strawberries

IN THE CUPBOARD
* salt
* pickled gherkins
* pickled capers
* Dijon mustard
* black peppercorns
* olive oil
* yellow Thai curry paste
* coconut milk
* sugar
* red wine vinegar

IN THE FRIDGE
* mayonnaise
* whipping cream,
  35% fat

Thai beef curry

Strawberries in vinegar

	Hours before the meal
	4
3½ hours before Make the curry (if using the oven method)	3½
	3
	2½
2 hours before Make the caramel and leave to cool. Add the vinegar and chill	2
1½ hours before Boil the potatoes for the salad, then wrap in foil and cool	1½
1 hour before Make the curry (if using a pressure cooker)	1
Mix the strawberries and vinegar caramel and leave to chill in the fridge	
30 minutes before Peel and chop the potatoes and prepare the salad ingredients	½
Just before eating Mix the dressing into the potatoes, sprinkle with the chives and serve	
Finish the Thai beef curry with the coconut milk and coriander	
	Start of the meal
Just before dessert Spoon the strawberries in vinegar into small bowls or glasses	
	Dessert

Potato salad

This German-style potato salad also makes a good accompaniment to a main meal or a good addition to a picnic.

•

Wrapping the potatoes in foil after cooking keeps them warm and makes them easier to peel.

	for 2	for 6	for 20	for 75
Large new potatoes	2	1.2 kg	4 kg	15 kg
Fresh chives, finely chopped	1 tsp	1½ tbsp	90 g	325 g
Small green onions (or use the white parts from a bunch of spring onions)	½	2	250 g	850 g
Medium pickled gherkins, drained	2	6	300 g	1 kg
Frankfurters	1	180 g	600 g	2 kg
Pickled capers, drained	2 tsp	1½ tbsp	300 g	1 kg
Mayonnaise	2 tbsp	360 g	1 kg	3.5 kg
Whipping cream, 35% fat	1½ tbsp	150 ml	300 g	900 g
Dijon mustard	1½ tbsp	135 g	400 g	1.3 kg

Start →

Bring a large pan of water to the boil, season with salt and add the potatoes. Cook for 20 minutes until tender.

Drain the potatoes and wrap individually in aluminium foil.

Meanwhile, finely chop the chives.

Trim the stalks off the onions.

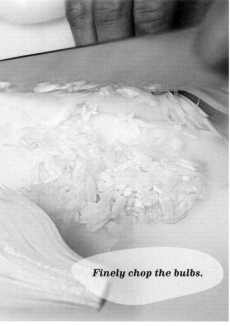

Finely chop the bulbs.

Cut the gherkins into 1-cm slices.

Continue →

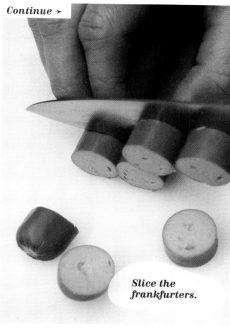

Slice the frankfurters.

Using a balloon whisk, mix together the mayonnaise, cream and mustard. Season with salt and pepper.

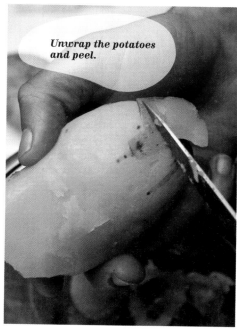

Unwrap the potatoes and peel.

Cut the potatoes into 3-cm cubes and put into a large bowl.

Add the onion, gherkin, capers and sausages to the potatoes.

Spoon the sauce on top, then mix together, taking care not to break up the potatoes.

Season the salad with salt and pepper.

Scatter with the chopped chives, and serve.

Thai beef curry

A pressure cooker is ideal
for cooking tough cuts of meat.
If you do not own a pressure
cooker, make the curry in the oven,
preheated to 160°C/325°F/Gas Mark 3.
Make the curry in a flameproof
casserole, then cover and cook in the
oven for 3 hours, until the beef is
very tender. Remove the beef,
then simmer the sauce until
thickened and tasty.

•

If you cannot find blade of beef,
try using shin, shank or cheek instead.

	for 2	for 6	for 20	for 75
Blade of beef	330 g	900 g	3 kg	12 kg
Olive oil	2 tbsp	80 ml	200 ml	500 ml
Fresh root ginger	½ tbsp	2 tsp	75 g	270 g
Yellow Thai curry paste	½ tsp	1 tsp	40 g	140 g
Fresh coriander, leaves picked	10 leaves	1 bunch	60 g	220 g
Coconut milk	100 ml	300 ml	1.3 l	5 l
Water	500 ml	1.5 l	3.4 l	13 l

Start →

Cut the beef into slices about 5 mm thick, to give 3 slices per person.

Season with salt and pepper.

Finely slice and then chop the ginger, without peeling it.

Place the base of the pressure cooker over a medium heat.

Add the oil, followed by the ginger. Fry gently for 2 minutes until fragrant.

Add the curry paste and stir through.

Continue →

Add half the coriander.

Add the water.

Next, add three-quarters of the coconut milk.

Add the beef.

Put the lid on the pressure cooker, then cook over a medium heat for 50 minutes. Remove the lid, then simmer until the sauce is thickened and tasty.

Add the rest of the coconut milk.

Add the remaining coriander leaves, then season to taste with salt if needed.

Serve the curry.

Strawberries in vinegar

We suggest Cabernet Sauvignon vinegar, but you could use balsamic vinegar instead if you like.

	for 2	for 6	for 20	for 75
Sugar	3 tbsp	175 g	600 g	2.2 kg
Boiling water	1 tbsp	65 ml	210 ml	800 ml
Red wine vinegar	2 tbsp	75 ml	240 ml	900 ml
Medium strawberries	10	600 g	2 kg	7.5 kg

Start →

Put the sugar into a wide saucepan and place the pan over a low-to-medium heat.

You will see darker patches of caramel starting to appear.

Stir to make an even, dark caramel.

Carefully pour in the boiling water using a metal ladle. The caramel will bubble dramatically, so take care not to burn yourself. Leave the caramel to cool a little.

Pour in the vinegar and mix well.

Continue →

Cool the caramel in the fridge. It will become quite thick.

Hull (remove the stalks and leaves from) the strawberries, then cut in half lengthways.

Put the strawberries into a bowl, then pour over the vinegar caramel.

Leave to marinate in the fridge for one hour before serving.

Farfalle with pesto

–

Japanese-style bream

–

Mandarins with Cointreau

INGREDIENTS

BUY FRESH
* gilthead bream
* green onions
* fresh coriander
* fresh root ginger
* mandarins

IN THE CUPBOARD
* salt
* farfalle
* extra-virgin olive oil
* sunflower oil
* soy sauce
* Cointreau
* demerara sugar

IN THE FRIDGE
* Parmesan cheese

IN THE FREEZER
* pesto sauce (see page 46)
* vanilla ice cream

Mandarins with Cointreau

Farfalle with pesto

Pesto sauce (see page 46) can be made ahead and frozen. Do not forget to defrost it in advance.

•

Before serving, add 2 tablespoons of the reserved cooking water to every 150 g of pesto. This helps to loosen and warm up the pesto.

•

You can use any kind of pasta shape you like.

	for 2	for 6	for 20	for 75
Water	1.5 l	3 l	6 l	22 l
Salt	1 pinch	2 pinches	60 g	500 g
Farfalle	200 g	600 g	2 kg	7.5 kg
Extra-virgin olive oil	3 tbsp	120 ml	400 ml	1.5 l
Pesto sauce (see page 46)	150 g	450 g	1.5 kg	5.5 kg
Parmesan cheese, finely grated	60 g	180 g	600 g	2 kg

Start →

Bring the water to the boil in a large pan. Season with the salt, then add the farfalle.

Stir once, then boil the pasta for 8–10 minutes until tender but still firm to the bite (check the instructions on the packet).

Grate the Parmesan cheese while you cook the pasta.

Reserve some of the cooking water. For 2 servings reserve 2 tablespoons of water, for 6 servings reserve 6 tablespoons, for 20 reserve 300 ml and for 75 reserve 1 l. Drain the pasta.

Tip the pasta back into its pan, then stir in the oil to prevent it sticking together.

Add the reserved cooking water to loosen the pesto, and stir well.

Serve the farfalle in a soup plate or shallow bowl.

Spoon over the pesto sauce.

Sprinkle Parmesan cheese over the top to serve.

Japanese-style bream

Ask your fishmonger to clean and gut the fish for you if you prefer.

•

You can grill the fish if you prefer.

•

You can use other kinds of fish, such as sea bass, hake or megrim.

	for 2	for 6	for 20	for 75
Gilthead bream, 350 g each	2	6	20	75
Green onions (or use the white parts of a bunch of spring onions) thinly sliced	1	2	300 g	1 kg
Sprigs fresh coriander	6	30	80 g	300 g
Fresh root ginger	20 g	60 g	200 g	750 g
Sunflower oil	3 tbsp	150 ml	400 ml	1.5 l
Soy sauce	1½ tbsp	4 tbsp	200 ml	750 ml

Start →

To scale the fish, run the back of a knife firmly along the length of the fish from the tail to the head.

Using kitchen scissors, cut the fins away from the body.

Cut along the belly from the small opening near the tail, to just under the head.

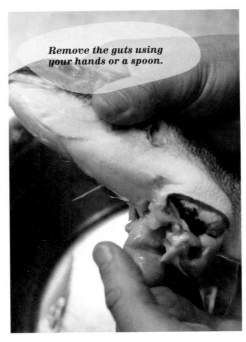

Remove the guts using your hands or a spoon.

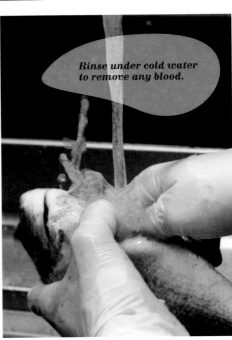

Rinse under cold water to remove any blood.

Make 3 deep cuts along the body of the fish.

Thinly slice the onion.

Pick the leaves from the coriander.

Thinly slice the ginger, without peeling it.

Continue ➜

Continue →

Wrap each fish loosely in a large square of baking parchment.

Fill the bottom of a steamer with water and bring it to the boil.

Season the fish with salt and steam for 12 minutes, until the flesh is opaque and flakes easily from the back bone.

While the fish is cooking, pour the oil into a saucepan with the ginger and cook over a medium heat until the ginger begins to fry.

Once the fish is cooked, transfer to a serving dish and scatter with the onion and coriander.

Carefully spoon over the hot ginger oil so that the onion and coriander start to sizzle.

Finish with a tablespoon of soy sauce.

Mandarins with Cointreau

To make scooping the ice cream easier,
take the tub out of the freezer
10 minutes beforehand
so that it softens a little.

•

If you cannot find mandarins, try using
satsumas or clementines, and Grand
Marnier can be substituted
for Cointreau.

	for 2	for 6	for 20	for 75
Mandarins	3	9	30	112
Cointreau	1½ tbsp	4 tbsp	80 ml	300 ml
Demerara sugar	1 tbsp	2 tbsp	65 g	200 g
Vanilla ice cream	2 scoops	6 scoops	500 g	2 kg

Start →

Squeeze the juice from one-third of the mandarins.

Peel the remaining fruit and break into segments.

Arrange the segments in a bowl in a flower shape, allowing one whole fruit per person. Spoon over the Cointreau.

Sprinkle with the sugar.

Pour over the mandarin juice.

Just before serving, place a quenelle or scoop of ice cream on top of the fruit.

Tomato & basil salad

–

Crab & rice stew

–

Coconut flan

Tomato & basil salad

INGREDIENTS

BUY FRESH
* very large ripe tomatoes
* fresh basil
* small whole crabs
* coconut milk
* desiccated or fresh coconut

IN THE CUPBOARD
* salt
* extra-virgin olive oil
* sherry vinegar
* olive oil
* paella rice
* white wine
* black peppercorns
* sugar

IN THE FRIDGE
* eggs

IN THE FREEZER
* fish stock (see page 56)
* sofrito (see page 43)
* picada (see page 41)

ORGANIZING THE MENU

	Hours before the meal
	4

Up to 4 hours before
Make the coconut crème caramel and chill in the fridge

	3½
	3
	2½
	2
	1½
	1
	½

30 minutes before
Brown the crabs and set aside. Start cooking the rice

While the rice is cooking, prepare the tomatoes for the salad and pick the basil

Just before eating
Finish the tomato salad with the oil and vinegar

	Start of the meal

Just before main course
Return the crabs to the rice and add the picada

	Main course

Just before dessert
Remove the flan from the moulds

	Dessert

Tomato & basil salad

–

This recipe is ideal when tomatoes are ripe in summer, although there are some varieties (such as Raf), which are still excellent in winter.

•

Use sea salt flakes to season the tomatoes if you prefer their flaky texture and slight crunch.

	for 2	for 6	for 20	for 75
Very large ripe tomatoes	3	9	2.5 kg	8 kg
Fresh basil	30 leaves	45 g	2 bunches	5 bunches
Extra-virgin olive oil	4 tbsp	180 ml	600 ml	2.2 l
Sherry vinegar	2 tsp	1½ tbsp	60 ml	150 ml

Start →

Using the tip of a small knife, remove the stalk and any fibrous green parts from the tops of the tomatoes.

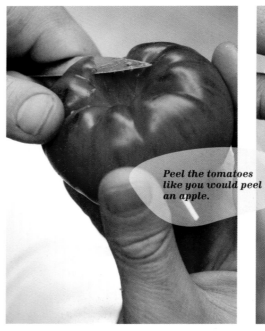

Peel the tomatoes like you would peel an apple.

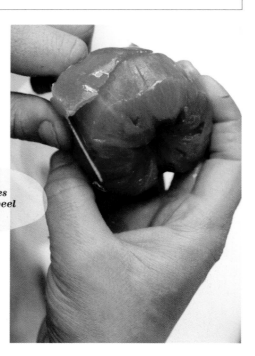

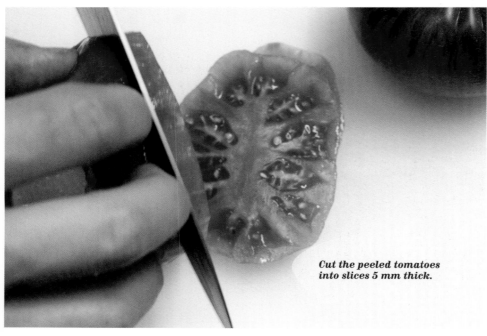

Cut the peeled tomatoes into slices 5 mm thick.

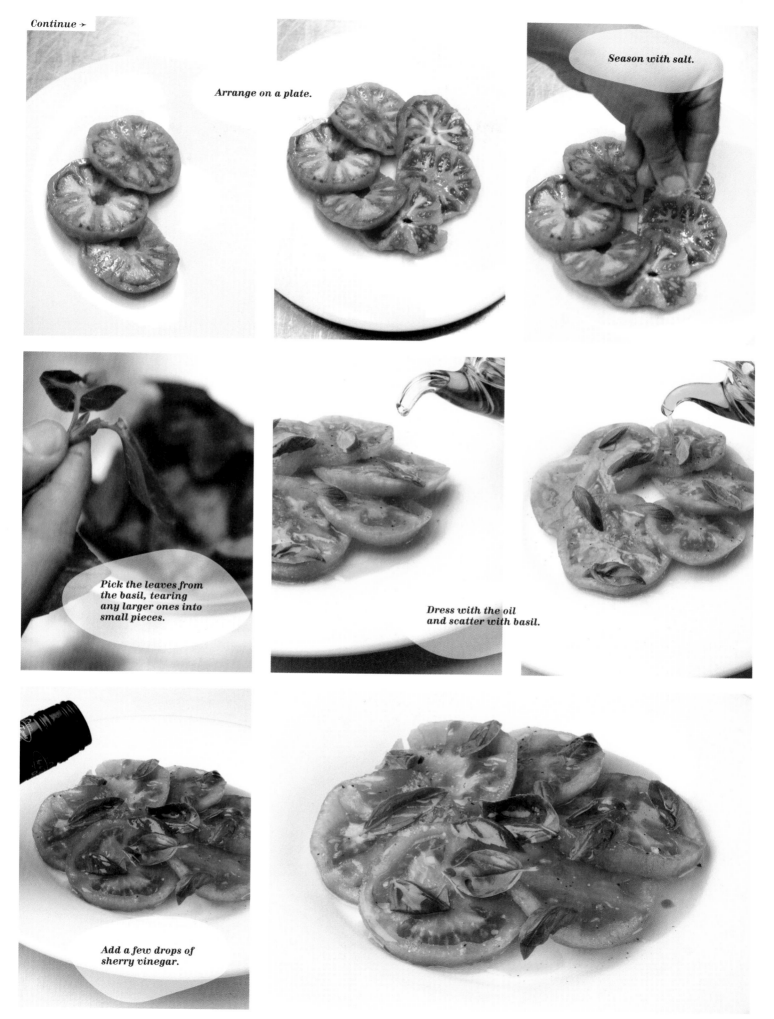

Continue →

Arrange on a plate.

Season with salt.

Pick the leaves from the basil, tearing any larger ones into small pieces.

Dress with the oil and scatter with basil.

Add a few drops of sherry vinegar.

Crab & rice stew

Small crabs are very delicate. Avoid stirring the rice once they have been added back to the pan, as the legs can easily break.

•

If the crabs are very small, remove the legs and only add the bodies, otherwise it could make eating this dish difficult.

•

You can use aioli (see page 53) instead of picada.

	for 2	for 6	for 20	for 75
Fish stock (see page 56)	1.2 l	3.6 l	9 l	30 l
Olive oil	1½ tbsp	100 ml	500 ml	1 l
Small whole crabs	15	700 g	2.5 kg	8.5 kg
Paella rice	200 g	600 g	2 kg	7.5 kg
Sofrito (see page 43)	1½ tbsp	100 g	300 g	1 kg
White wine	1½ tbsp	50 ml	150 ml	500 ml
Picada (see page 41)	2 tsp	2 tbsp	125 g	400 g

Start →

Pour the fish stock into a saucepan and bring to a simmer.

Put a large saucepan over a high heat, then add the oil. Add the crabs.

Fry the crabs until golden, then remove and set aside.

Reduce the heat slightly and add the sofrito to the same pan.

Add the rice.

Fry for 2 minutes, stirring to coat the rice in the sofrito.

Pour in the white wine, then scrape up any sediment from the bottom of the pan.

When most of the wine has boiled away, add a ladle of stock.

Once the stock has been absorbed, add another ladle and repeat the process for 3 minutes.

Add all the remaining stock to the rice, then simmer for 12 more minutes, stirring often.

Return the crabs to the pan. Season with salt and pepper.

Add the picada.

Serve the stew in shallow bowls.

Coconut flan

We do not recommend making less than the quantity given to serve 5. If you are serving fewer people, any leftover flan will keep in the fridge for up to 3 days.

•

You can use fresh or dessicated coconut.

•

You can also make the flans in small individual moulds or timbales, in which case reduce the cooking time to 15–20 minutes.

	for 2	for 5	for 20	for 75
For the caramel:				
Water	–	2 tsp	2 tbsp	100 ml
Sugar	–	30 g	100 g	1 kg
For the coconut flan:				
Eggs	–	2	8	32
Coconut milk	–	250 g	1 kg	4 kg
Grated coconut	–	15 g	60 g	450 g
Sugar	–	25 g	100 g	400 g

Start →

Preheat the oven to 180°C/ 350°F/Gas Mark 4.

Put the water and sugar into a saucepan over a low heat. Stir until the sugar has dissolved. Turn up the heat and boil to make a dark caramel.

Divide the caramel between individual or large moulds and set aside to cool.

Break the eggs into a large bowl, then whisk until frothy.

Put the coconut milk, grated coconut and sugar into another large bowl and whisk until the sugar dissolves. Save any leftover coconut milk for serving later.

Add the eggs and whisk until even.

Pour the mixture into the caramel-filled moulds.

Cover the tops of the moulds with foil, then transfer to a roasting tin.

Pour enough cold water into the roasting tin to come half-way up the sides of the moulds. Bake for 30 minutes, making sure the water does not boil.

Once the crème caramel is cooked (it will be just firm to the touch), leave to cool in the water. Remove from the water and chill in the fridge.

When ready to serve, loosen the flan with a round-bladed knife.

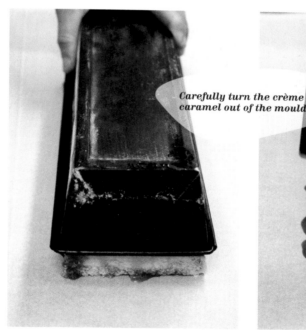

Carefully turn the crème caramel out of the moulds.

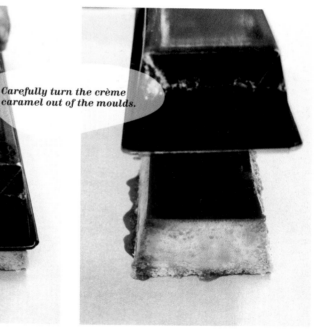

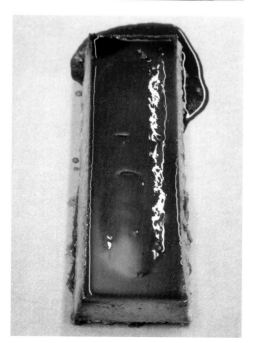

Slice into 2-cm slices.

Serve the slices surrounded with a few spoons of coconut milk.

–

Meal 15

–

Bread & garlic soup

–

Mexican-style slow-cooked pork

–

Figs with cream & kirsch

INGREDIENTS

BUY FRESH
* white country-style
  loaf
* boned and tied
  pork shoulder joint
* red onions
* small habanero
  chillies
* figs
* oranges
* limes

IN THE CUPBOARD
* olive oil
* garlic
* salt
* black peppercorns
* mild paprika
* dried oregano
* ground cumin
* white wine vinegar
* *achiote* paste
* onions
* flour tortillas
* kirsch
* sugar

IN THE FRIDGE
* eggs
* whipping cream,
  35% fat

IN THE FREEZER
* chicken stock
  (see page 57)

Figs with cream & kirsch

ORGANIZING THE MENU

	Hours before the meal

Up to 24 hours before
Make the marinade for the pork and leave to marinate

4 hours before _____ 4
Put the pork in the oven

3½

3

2½

2

1½

1

30 minutes before _____ ½
Make the bread and garlic soup

Chop the red onions and chillies for the pork

Prepare the figs and put into bowls. Splash with a little kirsch

Whip the cream and kirsch, and keep in the fridge

5 minutes before _____
Cook the eggs to your liking, then serve with the soup

Shred the pork shoulder and place on a serving dish

Toast the tortillas in a frying pan _____ **Start of the meal**

Just before dessert _____
Spoon the kirsch cream onto the figs to serve

Dessert

Bread & garlic soup

This dish is good topped with either a boiled or poached egg, or we sometimes cook the egg in its shell in a low-temperature water bath called a Roner. This gives a very soft and silky result. To boil, as well as poach an egg, see page 21.

•

Spanish *choricero* pepper paste can be used instead of paprika. It is available from specialist Spanish food shops and delicatessens.

	for 2	for 6	for 20	for 75
Olive oil	80 ml	240 ml	800 ml	3 l
500-g white country-style loaf, cut into 50-g slices	4 slices	12 slices	800 g	3 kg
Garlic cloves	2	6	180 g	600 g
Mild paprika	2 tsp	4 tsp	8 g	25 g
Chicken stock (see page 57)	450 ml	1.5 l	4.5 l	16 l
Eggs	2	6	20	75

Start →

Place a frying pan over a medium heat, then add half the oil. When it is hot, add the bread.

Fry until well browned all over. Remove the slices from the oil.

Roughly crush the garlic.

Place a large saucepan over a medium heat, then pour in the remaining oil. Add the garlic and fry until golden.

Once the garlic has turned golden, add the paprika.

Add the fried bread and chicken stock.

Season with salt and pepper.

Simmer for 20 minutes, then process with a hand-held blender.

Meanwhile, cook the eggs to your liking (see note).

The soup will be smooth and tasty.

Serve the soup with the cooked egg.

Mexican-style slow-cooked pork

The original name of this dish is *cochinita pibil*, and it comes from Mexico's Yucatan Peninsula. Cider vinegar is used in Mexico instead of white wine vinegar.

•

If you have time, marinate the pork shoulder for 12 hours in the fridge. If you are short of time, you can marinate it for 30 minutes.

•

Achiote (or annatto) is a shrub native to Mexico and Peru. Its fruit is used as a colouring and flavouring in many dishes. The paste is available from specialist food shops and delicatessens. If you cannot find it, you could try making a mixture of orange and lemon juice, pepper and saffron, although the results will be different.

•

You can use flour or corn tortillas.

	for 2	for 6	for 20	for 75
Orange juice	50 ml	150 ml	500 ml	1.5 l
Dried oregano	A pinch	2 pinches	½ tsp	2 tsp
Ground cumin	A pinch	2 pinches	0.6 g	2 g
White wine vinegar	2 tsp	2 tbsp	80 ml	300 ml
Achiote paste	60 g	180 g	600 g	2 kg
Olive oil	1½ tbsp	4 tbsp	150 ml	500 ml
Boned and tied pork shoulder joint	350g	1 kg	3.5 kg	12 kg
Salt	A pinch	2 pinches	150 g	500 g
Onions	¼	1	125 g	350 g
Red onions	½	2	750 g	2.5 kg
Small habanero chillies	¼	½	1	2
Lime juice	1 tbsp (½ lime)	3 tbsp (1 lime)	60 ml	200 ml
Flour tortillas	2	6	20	75

For 2 people you will need 1 orange and ½ lime. For 6 people you will need 2 oranges and 1 lime.

Start →

In a small bowl, whisk together the the orange juice, oregano, cumin, white wine vinegar, achiote paste and oil.

Process with a hand-held blender until smooth.

Prick the meat several times with a fine-pointed knife to help the marinade to penetrate deep into the meat. Season with salt and pepper.

Continue →

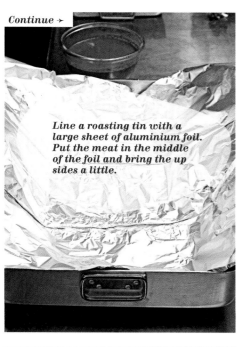

Line a roasting tin with a large sheet of aluminium foil. Put the meat in the middle of the foil and bring the up sides a little.

Pour over the marinade.

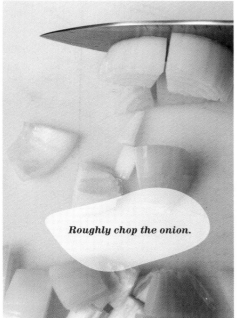

Roughly chop the onion.

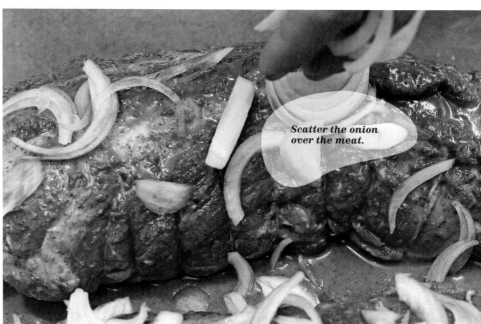

Scatter the onion over the meat.

Preheat the oven to 200°C/400°F/Gas Mark 6.

Fold the foil over the meat to make a parcel and seal the edges tightly, so that no steam or liquid will escape as it cooks. Leave to marinate for a minimum of 30 minutes.

Cook the pork shoulder for 4 hours. While it cooks, finely chop the red onion.

Continue →

Continue →

Remove the seeds from the habanero chilli and chop the flesh finely.

Mix the chilli with the onion. Add the lime juice, then season with salt.

Once cooked, take the meat out of the oven and let it rest for 20 minutes.

While you wait, toast the tortillas in a dry frying pan and wrap in foil to keep warm.

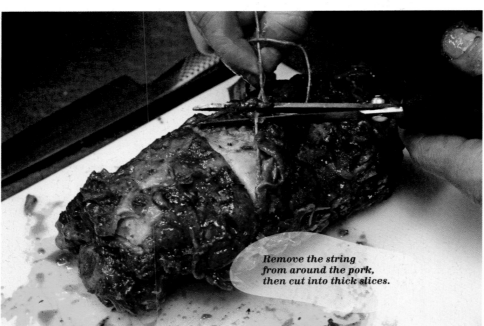

Remove the string from around the pork, then cut into thick slices.

Spread the pork over a serving platter and pull the meat to shreds with your fingers.

Spoon over the sauce from the pan.

Serve the pork with the warm tortillas and red onion salsa.

Figs with cream & kirsch

Kirsch is a cherry brandy with a high alcohol content. It is typical of Germany, Switzerland, Austria and regions in France such as Alsace and Franche-Comté.

•

If no kirsch is available, use another white spirit, such as maraschino liqueur or white rum.

	for 2	for 6	for 20	for 75
Ripe figs	3	9	35	120
Kirsch, for the figs	2 tsp	2 tbsp	4 tbsp	250 ml
Whipping cream, 35% fat	4 tbsp	180 ml	600 ml	2 l
Sugar	1 tsp	1½ tbsp	80 g	300 g
Kirsch, for the cream	1 tsp	2 tsp	1 tbsp	50 ml

Start →

Cut each fig into 4 wedges.

Arrange 6 fig wedges in each serving bowl, then drizzle with the first quantity of kirsch.

Using a balloon whisk, whip the cream with the sugar to soft peaks.

Add the second quantity of kirsch, and then whip the cream a little more until it thickens up again.

Spoon the cream over the figs to serve.

Noodles with shiitake & ginger

–

Duck with chimichurri sauce

–

Pistachio custard

INGREDIENTS

BUY FRESH
* bacon
* small green onions
* fresh root ginger
* beansprouts
* duck breasts

IN THE CUPBOARD
* dried shiitake
  mushrooms
* oyster sauce
* soy sauce
* Chinese Shaoxing wine
* sesame oil
* medium egg noodles
* olive oil
* *shichimi togarashi*
  spice mix
* salt
* black peppercorns
* sugar
* shelled pistachios

IN THE FRIDGE
* chimichurri sauce
  (see page 51)
* eggs
* whole milk
* whipping cream
  35% fat

Duck with chimichurri sauce

Pistachio custard

ORGANIZING THE MENU	Hours before the meal
The day before Soak the shiitake mushrooms in water	4
	3½
	3
	2½
2 hours before Make the custard and chill in the fridge	2
	1½
	1
30 minutes before Boil the noodles, then chill in iced water	½
Prepare the rest of the noodle ingredients	
20 minutes before Brown the duck, wrap in foil and leave to rest	
Fry the bacon for the noodles, then cook the ginger, mushrooms and onions	
5 minutes before Add the drained noodles and beansprouts to the vegetables, fry for 5 minutes, then add the sauce	
	Start of the meal
Just before main course Slice the duck and arrange in a serving dish with the chimichurri	
	Main course

Noodles with shiitake & ginger

At elBulli, we often use ginger oil instead of fresh ginger.

•

Shichimi togarashi is a mix of seven spices used in Japanese cooking and characterized by its hot flavour. If you cannot find it at the shops, use freshly ground black pepper and a little chilli powder instead.

•

Shaoxing rice wine, shiitake mushrooms, *shichimi togarashi*, oyster sauce and the noodles can all be purchased from shops specializing in Asian food, and from some larger supermarkets.

	for 2	for 6	for 20	for 75
Dried shiitake mushrooms	6	80 g	160 g	600 g
Oyster sauce	3 tsp	100 g	400 g	1.4 kg
Soy sauce	3 tsp	100 ml	350 ml	1.4 l
Chinese Shaoxing rice wine	3 tsp	100 ml	350 ml	1.4 l
Sesame oil	1 tbsp	60 ml	180 ml	650 ml
Medium egg noodles	120 g	360 g	1.2 kg	4 kg
Bacon	80 g	240 g	800 g	3 kg
Small green onions, roughly chopped (or use the white parts from a bunch of spring onions)	1	2	1.2 kg	4 kg
Fresh root ginger, finely chopped	1 tsp	20 g	30 g	100 g
Beansprouts	35 g	100 g	350 g	1.2 kg
Olive oil	2 tsp	2 tbsp	300 ml	1 l
Shichimi togarashi	1 pinch	2 pinches	6 g	20 g

Start →

Put the shiitake mushrooms into a large bowl, cover with plenty of cold water and leave to soak for 12 hours.

Continue →

Once soaked, the mushrooms will be soft. Remove the stems.

Slice the caps into strips.

Pour the oyster sauce into a bowl.

Add the soy sauce, Shaoxing wine and sesame oil.

Mix with a balloon whisk.

Fill a bowl with iced water and add salt.

Bring a pan of water to the boil, then add the noodles. Cook the noodles until tender, about 3½ minutes (check the instructions on the packet).

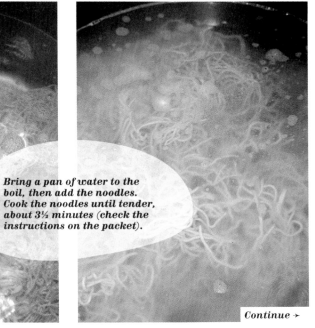

Continue →

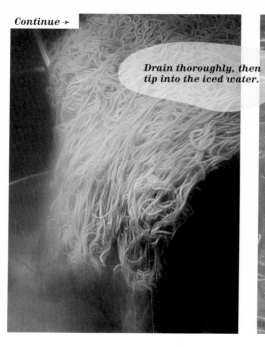

Continue →

Drain thoroughly, then tip into the iced water.

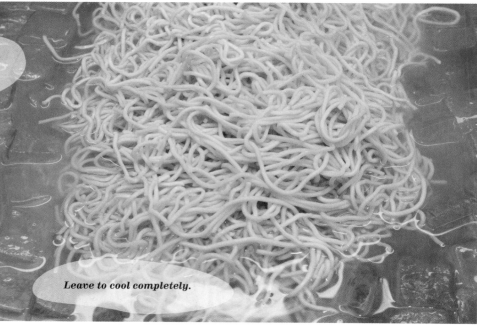

Leave to cool completely.

Slice the excess fat off the bacon.

Cut into thin strips.

Roughly chop the green onion and select the best beansprouts. Discard any that are not fresh.

Peel the ginger using a teaspoon.

Slice and finely chop the ginger.

Heat the oil in a large pan or wok, then add the bacon and fry until golden brown.

Continue →

Add the chopped ginger and shiitake mushrooms and fry for 1–2 minutes.

Add the onions and fry until browned, stirring frequently.

Drain the noodles. Add the beansprouts and noodles to the pan.

Stir-fry for 5 minutes, then add the soy sauce mixture, mixing well to coat the noodles.

Serve the noodles on a plate, then sprinkle with a little shichimi togarashi.

Duck with chimichurri sauce

Chimichurri is a sauce made from parsley, garlic, spices, olive oil and vinegar (see page 51). It comes from South America, where it is often served with steak, but it is also good with duck.

	for 2	for 6	for 20	for 75
Duck breasts	1	3	8	25
Chimichurri sauce (see page 51)	110 g	340 g	1.1 kg	4 kg

Start →

Score the duck skin with a very sharp knife, to make a grid of 1-cm squares. Take care not to cut through the flesh. Season with salt and pepper.

Heat a large frying pan over a high heat, then add the duck, skin side down. Fry for 3 minutes, until browned.

Turn the duck over and cook for 30 seconds on the flesh side before removing from the heat.

Wrap the duck in a sheet of foil and leave to rest for 15 minutes.

Cut the breast into slices about 3 mm thick, then overlap the slices on a dish.

Season with salt and pepper, then spoon over the chimichurri sauce.

Pistachio custard

If you have a kitchen thermometer, use it to check when the custard is ready – it will thicken at 80°C (170°F). If you do not have a thermometer, check the back of the spoon: the custard is ready when it is thick enough to coat it.

	for 2	for 6	for 20	for 75
Whole milk	200 ml	600 ml	2 l	8 l
Whipping cream, 35% fat	50 ml	150 ml	500 ml	2 l
Egg yolks	2	6	400 g	1.6 kg
Sugar	45 g	135 g	450 g	1.8 kg
Shelled pistachios	35 g	105 g	350 g	1.4 kg

Start →

Pour the milk and cream into a saucepan and bring to the boil.

Meanwhile, whisk together the egg yolks and sugar in a large bowl.

Pour in the hot milk and cream, whisking continuously.

Pour the mixture back into the pan over a low heat. Cook for 5–10 minutes, stirring frequently with a spatula, until thickened.

Put the pistachios into a bowl and pour in the hot custard.

Process in a food processor or with a hand-held blender until very smooth and creamy.

Pour into small glasses or serving bowls and chill thoroughly in the fridge.

Baked potatoes with romesco sauce

–

Whiting in salsa verde

–

Rice pudding

INGREDIENTS

BUY FRESH
* small new potatoes
* fresh whole whiting
* fresh parsley
* lemons

IN THE CUPBOARD
* small onions
* garlic
* salt
* extra-virgin olive oil
* flour
* pudding rice
* sugar
* ground cinnamon

IN THE FRIDGE
* whole milk
* butter
* whipping cream,
  35% fat

IN THE FREEZER
* romesco sauce (see
  page 45)
* fish stock (see page
  56)

Rice pudding

	Hours before the meal
	4
	3½
	3
	2½
	2
At least 1 hour before Cook the rice pudding and chill in the fridge	1½
1 hour before Bake the potatoes and onions	1
Cut the fish into pieces and chop the garlic and parsley	½
25 minutes before Cook the whiting in salsa verde	
Just before eating Cut the baked potatoes and onions in half	
	Start of the meal
Just before main course Arrange the fish on a plate and cover with the salsa verde	
Just before dessert Sprinkle cinnamon over the rice pudding	Main course
	Dessert

Baked potatoes with romesco sauce

Romesco is a traditional sauce from Tarragona in Catalonia. It is made from hazelnuts, red peppers, sherry vinegar and olive oil, and it is usually served with seafood, vegetables or chicken.

	for 2	for 6	for 20	for 75
Small new potatoes	4	12	3 kg	10 kg
Small onions, left in their skins	2	6	2 kg	7.5 kg
Romesco sauce (see page 45)	130 g	400 g	1.3 kg	5 kg

Start →

Preheat the oven to 200°C/ 400°F/Gas Mark 6. Wrap each potato in aluminium foil.

Place the potatoes and onions in a roasting tin. Bake for 35–45 minutes.

When ready, the potatoes and onions will be tender, and the onion skins will be charred in places.

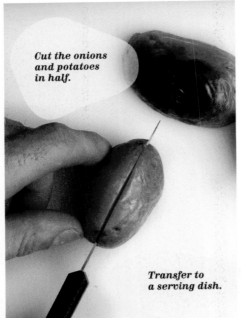

Cut the onions and potatoes in half.

Transfer to a serving dish.

Season with salt to taste and spoon the sauce over the hot vegetables.

Whiting in salsa verde

Ask your fishmonger to clean and gut the fish for you if you prefer.

•

You can use other kinds of white fish in this recipe, such as sea bream or even shellfish. Cook in the sauce for 3–5 minutes.

	for 2	for 6	for 20	for 75
Fresh whole whiting, cleaned and gutted, 250 g each	2	6	20	75
Salt	1 pinch	2 pinches	25 g	100 g
Garlic cloves, finely chopped	1	3	40 g	130 g
Fresh parsley, finely chopped	1½ tbsp	4 tbsp	1 bunch	3 bunches
Extra-virgin olive oil	1½ tbsp	5 tbsp	350 ml	1 l
Flour	1 tsp	1½ tbsp	80 g	200 g
Water	175 ml	500 ml	1.5 l	4 l

Start →

Cut the heads from the whiting, then cut the each body into two equal pieces. Season with a little of the salt.

To make the salsa verde, first finely chop the garlic.

Place a large pan over a low heat, then pour in the oil. Add the garlic and fry it gently for 1–2 minutes until softened but not browned.

Finely chop the parsley.

Continue →

Continue →

Stir the flour into the oil and garlic, and fry for 30 seconds. Add half the chopped parsley.

Pour in the water.

Simmer the sauce for 10 minutes, stirring occasionally, until it thickens slightly.

Place the fish in the sauce and simmer for 10 minutes, until the flesh flakes easily.

Season the sauce with salt, then scatter with the rest of the parsley.

Lift the fish onto serving plates, then spoon over the salsa verde.

Rice pudding

Rice pudding is a common dessert in many European, Latin American and Asian countries. The cooking method is universal – what sets the recipes apart is the flavourings used, which can include vanilla, cinnamon, lemon zest, *dulce de leche* (milk caramel), saffron, cardamom or port.

•

You could use any round-grained rice for this recipe.

	for 2	for 6	for 20	for 75
Whole milk	320 ml	1 l	3.5 l	13 l
Whipping cream, 35% fat	4 tbsp	175 ml	800 ml	2.8 l
Lemon zest in 5-cm strips	1 strip	2 strips	½ lemon	1 lemon
Cinnamon sticks	¼	½	1	2
Pudding rice	80 g	240 g	800 g	3 kg
Butter	20 g	60 g	200 g	700 g
Sugar	50 g	135 g	600 g	1.8 kg
Ground cinnamon	1 pinch	2 pinches	20 g	70 g

Start →

Pour the milk and cream into a large saucepan.

Add the lemon zest and cinnamon sticks and leave to infuse for 5 minutes.

Pour half the infused milk and cream into another saucepan. Add the rice and cook over a low heat for 45 minutes, adding the remaining milk and cream gradually, stirring frequently, as if making risotto.

Add the sugar 10 minutes after the mixture starts to boil. Stir occasionally to prevent sticking.

Once the rice is tender and creamy, add the butter and stir it in.

Spoon the rice into bowls, cool, then chill in the fridge.

Just before serving, sprinkle ground cinnamon over the rice pudding.

Guacamole with tortilla chips

–

Mexican-style chicken with rice

–

Watermelon with menthol sweets

BUY FRESH
* ripe tomatoes
* avocados
* fresh coriander
* lemons
* chicken leg quarters
* watermelon

IN THE CUPBOARD
* salt
* tortilla chips
* sesame seeds
* onions
* olive oil
* paella rice
* red mole paste
* tinned sweetcorn
* black peppercorns
* sugar
* hard menthol throat
  sweets
* N$_2$O cartridges for
  the siphon

IN THE FRIDGE
* butter

–
*Guacamole
with
tortilla chips*
–

–
*Mexican-style
chicken
with rice*
–

Watermelon with menthol sweets

ORGANIZING THE MENU	Hours before the meal
	4
	3½
	3
	2½
	2
1½ hours before Simmer the chicken leg quarters	1½
Make the mole sauce	1
Prepare the tomatoes and onion for the guacamole. Purée the onion and coriander for the rice	
30 minutes before Cut up the watermelon, marinate in the syrup and chill in the fridge	½
Crush the throat sweets	
Cover the chicken with the sauce and cook in the oven	
20 minutes before Cook the Mexican rice	
While the rice and chicken are cooking, finish the guacamole	
Just before eating Finish the rice with the sweetcorn, butter and coriander	
	Start of the meal
Just before dessert Drain the watermelon and place on a serving dish	
	Dessert

Guacamole with tortilla chips

When making guacamole in small quantities you can also use a pestle and mortar, which is the traditional method.

•

If the tomatoes are very ripe, you may not need to scald them before peeling.

	for 2	for 6	for 20	for 75
Ripe tomatoes, diced	1 tbsp	2 tbsp	400 g	1.2 kg
Avocados	1	3	2 kg	7 kg
Medium onion, finely chopped	1 tbsp	3 tbsp	120 g	400 g
Fresh coriander, finely chopped	1½ tbsp	4 tbsp	25 g	100 g
Lemon juice	1½ tbsp	4 tbsp	150 ml	500 ml
Salt	1 pinch	1 generous pinch	¼ tsp	2 tsp
Tortilla chips	100 g	250 g	700 g	2.5 kg

To make it for 2 people you will need to buy 1 tomato and 1 onion; for 6, you will need 2 tomatoes and 1 onion.

Start →

Fill a saucepan with water, then bring to the boil.

Cut a cross into the underside of each tomato with a knife. Fill a bowl with iced water.

Put the tomatoes into the boiling water and leave for 10 seconds.

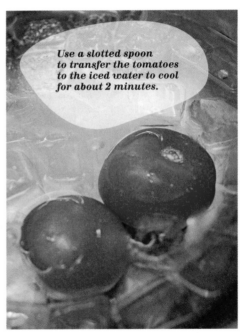

Use a slotted spoon to transfer the tomatoes to the iced water to cool for about 2 minutes.

Once cooled, peel the skin off the tomatoes. You could use the tip of a knife to help if necessary.

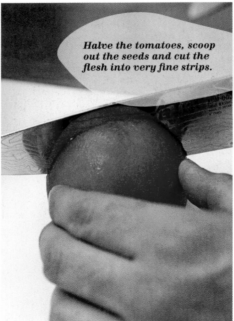

Halve the tomatoes, scoop out the seeds and cut the flesh into very fine strips.

Dice into cubes.

Pick the leaves off the coriander stalks and chop them finely.

Cut the avocados in half and remove the stones. Remove the flesh with a spoon.

Mash the avocado using a whisk, fork or hand-held blender.

Chop the onion finely.

Add the chopped tomato, onion and coriander to the avocados.

Pour in the lemon juice and stir. Season with salt.

Serve the guacamole with tortilla chips.

Mexican-style chicken with rice

Mole is a Mexican sauce containing chilli and spices, which usually accompanies meat.

•

There are many varieties of mole sauces, which differ according to the type of chilli and other ingredients. Mole pastes are available from specialist shops and delicatessens.

•

When making it for 20 or 75, you could add 0.6 g Xanthan (see page 11) for every litre of sauce, to help thicken it.

	for 2	for 6	for 20	for 75
Chicken legs (thigh and drumstick connected)	2	6	20	75
Water	600 ml	1.2 l	6 l	18 l
Sprigs fresh coriander	5	8	30 g	100 g
Salt	1 pinch	2 pinches	1 tsp	40 g
Red mole paste	100 g	300 g	1 kg	3.5 kg
Sesame seeds	2 tsp	2 tbsp	60 g	200 g

Start →

Place the chicken legs in a large pan, cover with water and add the salt.

Add the coriander sprigs.

Bring to the boil and simmer the chicken for 45 minutes, topping up with more hot water if necessary, to ensure the chicken is covered.

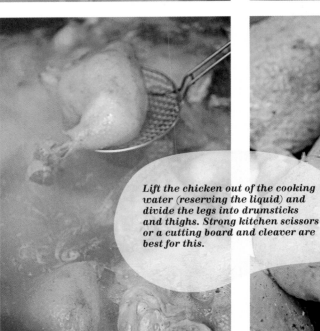

Lift the chicken out of the cooking water (reserving the liquid) and divide the legs into drumsticks and thighs. Strong kitchen scissors or a cutting board and cleaver are best for this.

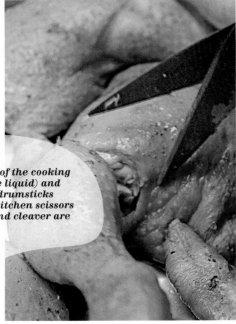

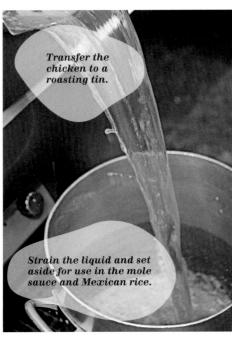

Transfer the chicken to a roasting tin.

Strain the liquid and set aside for use in the mole sauce and Mexican rice.

Continue →

Preheat the oven to 160°C/325°F/ Gas Mark 3.

Spoon the mole paste into a saucepan. Stir over a low heat until it begins to melt.

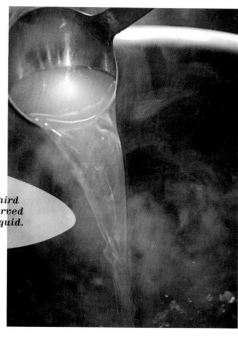

Add one-third of the reserved chicken liquid.

Boil for 15 minutes until the sauce has a creamy consistency.

Cover the chicken with the sauce and roast for 30 minutes until the sauce is thick and tasty, and the chicken is very tender. To check, insert the tip of a sharp knife into the chicken flesh.

Meanwhile, toast the sesame seeds in a frying pan over a low heat, stirring frequently. Tip out of the pan as soon as they are ready.

Arrange the chicken on a serving dish. Cover with the sauce, then sprinkle with the toasted sesame seeds.

Serve with Mexican rice (page 244).

Mexican rice

Perfect as a side dish with Mexican-style chicken (see page 242), this dish also works as a starter with a few slices of avocado.

•

If you do not have a blender you can finely chop the onion and coriander instead of puréeing it.

	for 2	for 6	for 20	for 75
Chicken stock (from the Mexican-style chicken recipe, page 242)	500 ml	1.5 l	5 l	16 l
Small onions, roughly chopped	½	1½	400 g	1.2 kg
Sprigs fresh coriander	2	1 handful	120 g	400 g
Olive oil	2 tbsp	4 tbsp	150 ml	500 ml
Paella rice	150 g	450 g	1.5 kg	5 kg
Tinned sweetcorn, drained	50 g	150 g	225 g	800 g
Butter	1 tbsp	50 g	150 g	500 g

Start →

Pour the chicken stock into a saucepan and bring to a simmer. Meanwhile use a hand-held blender to purée the onion and half of the coriander to make a smooth paste.

Pour the oil into a large saucepan over a medium heat. Add the rice and cook for 1 minute, stirring.

Add the onion and coriander mixture to the rice and continue to fry gently for 2 minutes.

Pour in the hot stock and simmer the rice for 20 minutes, stirring occasionally to prevent sticking.

Meanwhile, finely chop the remaining coriander.

When the rice is nearly cooked (after about 17 minutes), add the drained sweetcorn.

When the time is up, turn off the heat. Add the butter and stir until the rice has a creamy texture.

Add the chopped coriander, season with salt and pepper, and serve.

Watermelon with menthol sweets

Our sense of taste perceives four basic flavours; sweet, salty, sour and bitter, plus a series of nuances, collectively called 'mouthfeel'. Among these nuances is menthol, which gives the palate a feeling of freshness and works very well in this dish. Others include astringency, spiciness, tartness and effervescence.

•

If you have a vacuum-packing machine, seal the watermelon and lemon syrup in a vacuum-pack bag. This will allow the liquid to penetrate more thoroughly into the fruit.

	for 2	for 6	for 20	for 75
Lemon juice	1½ tbsp	3 tbsp	300 ml	1 l
Sugar	2 tbsp	6 tbsp	300 g	1 kg
Watermelon	1 wedge	½	1½	5
Hard menthol throat sweets	4	12	200 g	750 g

Start →

Strain the lemon juice into a bowl and add the sugar. Stir to dissolve.

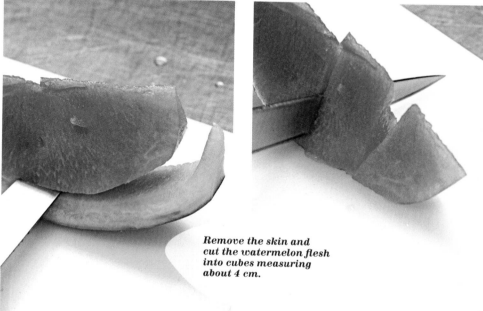

Remove the skin and cut the watermelon flesh into cubes measuring about 4 cm.

Transfer the melon and lemon syrup into a food bag or non-reactive bowl, then leave to marinate in the fridge for 30 minutes.

Put the sweets between two sheets of baking parchment and crush with a rolling pin or other heavy utensil to make a fine powder.

Drain the watermelon pieces and arrange on a serving dish. You can serve it on crushed ice, if you like.

Serve the melon with the crushed sweets in a separate bowl, for guests to sprinkle.

Spaghetti with tomato & basil

–

Fried fish with garlic

–

Caramel foam

INGREDIENTS

BUY FRESH
* fresh basil
* fresh whole fish, cleaned and gutted

IN THE CUPBOARD
* salt
* spaghetti
* extra-virgin olive oil
* olive oil
* garlic
* sherry vinegar
* sugar
* N_2O cartridges for the siphon

IN THE FRIDGE
* whipping cream, 35% fat
* Parmesan cheese
* whole milk
* eggs

IN THE FREEZER
* tomato sauce (see page 42)

ORGANIZING THE MENU	Hours before the meal
	4
	3½
	3
	2½
2 hours before _____ Make the caramel base for the foam	2
Fill the siphon and chill in the fridge or in an ice bucket	1½
	1
30 minutes before _____ Trim the fins and remove the head from the fish	½
Reheat the tomato sauce	
Fry the garlic and make the garlic dressing for the fish	
10 minutes before _____ Boil the spaghetti	___
5 minutes before _____ Cook the fish	___
Just before eating _____ Drain the pasta and toss with the oil	___
Put the fish onto a serving plate, cover with the fried garlic and spoon over the dressing _____	
	Start of the meal
Just before dessert Dispense the caramel foam into small bowls _____	
	Dessert

Spaghetti with tomato & basil

The tomato sauce (see page 42)
can be made ahead and frozen
(or use a quality shop-bought sauce instead).
Do not forget to defrost it in advance.

•

As well as flavouring the pasta, the
oil prevents the spaghetti strands from
sticking together, which is especially
useful for large quantities.

•

When cooking pasta, add 10 g salt
per litre of water.

	for 2	for 6	for 20	for 75
Tomato sauce (see page 42)	200 g	600 g	2 kg	7 kg
Fresh basil	20 leaves	60 leaves	60 g	200 g
Water	600 ml	2 l	15 l	60 l
Salt	1 tsp	1¼ tsp	150 g	600 g
Spaghetti	200 g	600 g	2 kg	7 kg
Extra-virgin olive oil	3 tbsp	120 ml	400 ml	1.5 l
Parmesan cheese	30 g	90 g	600 g	2 kg

Start →

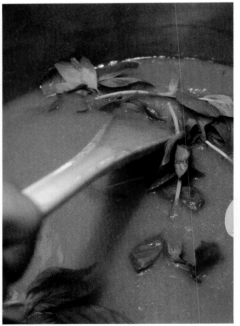

In a saucepan over medium heat, bring the tomato sauce to a simmer.

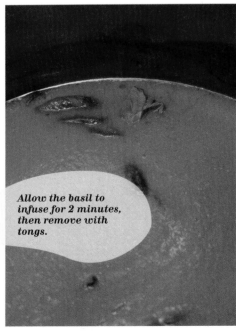

Pick the basil leaves from their stems and set aside the smallest and best ones for finishing the dish.

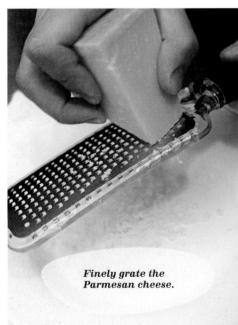

Remove the tomato sauce from the heat and stir in the rest of the basil.

Allow the basil to infuse for 2 minutes, then remove with tongs.

Finely grate the Parmesan cheese.

Bring the water to the boil in a large pot. Add the salt and spaghetti. Stir once or twice to prevent sticking.

Boil for 8–10 minutes or until tender but still firm to the bite (check the instructions on the packet).

Tip the pasta into a colander and drain well.

Transfer the pasta to a large serving dish and stir in the olive oil.

Using tongs or a wooden fork, divide the spaghetti onto serving plates.

Spoon the tomato sauce over the top.

Scatter with the remaining basil leaves.

Finish with the grated Parmesan.

Fried fish with garlic

Ask your fishmonger to clean
and gut the fish for you if you prefer.

•

At elBulli we use a large flat griddle,
but at home a large flat frying pan is fine.

•

Almost any small fish can be used
for this dish. For thicker fish the cooking
time should be longer – it should be golden
on both sides and tender and juicy
in the middle.

	for 2	for 6	for 20	for 75
Fresh whole fish, cleaned and gutted, 175–250 g each	2	6	20	75
Garlic cloves	3	9	100 g	375 g
Olive oil	4 tbsp, plus extra to cook the fish	150 ml, plus extra to cook the fish	650 ml, plus extra to cook the fish	2.5 l, plus extra to cook the fish
Sherry vinegar	2 tsp	2 tbsp	150 ml	150 ml

Start →

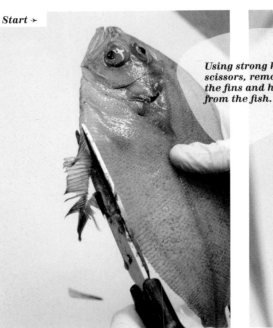

Using strong kitchen scissors, remove the fins and head from the fish.

Peel the garlic and slice very finely, using a mandolin or sharp knife.

Pour the oil into a small pan and add the garlic.

Put the pan over a medium heat and gently fry the garlic until golden. Take care, as garlic can easily burn.

Drain the garlic through a fine-meshed metal sieve, reserving the oil.

Continue →

Tip the garlic onto kitchen paper and let the paper absorb any excess oil.

Allow the oil to cool a little, then add the sherry vinegar and stir to make a dressing.

Season the fish with salt. Heat a large frying pan or flat griddle, add a little oil and place the fish in it.

Fry the fish for 1 minute, or until golden underneath. Use a fish slice to turn the fish.

Cook on the second side for 1 minute, then transfer to a serving dish.

Scatter the fried garlic over the fish. Give the oil-and-vinegar dressing a final stir.

Spoon a couple of tablespoons of dressing over each fish.

Caramel foam

A siphon is a restaurant tool that is definitely worth buying for home use. If you do not have a siphon, make caramel ice cream instead: follow this recipe and freeze the mixture in an ice-cream machine.

•

You can add your choice of topping to the foam, such as toffee sauce or crushed hard toffees.

•

If you are making this for more than 6–8 people, heat the milk and cream together before pouring into the caramel, to avoid too much splashing.

	for 2	for 6–8	for 20	for 75
Sugar	-	60 g	160 g	600 g
Whipping cream, 35% fat	-	320 ml	640 ml	2.4 l
Whole milk	-	6 tbsp	180 ml	600 ml
Egg yolks	-	4	225 g	720 g
N₂O cartridges for the siphon	-	2	4	14

The minimum quantity of foam you can make in a siphon is 6–8 portions.
For 6–8 you will need a 0.5-litre siphon.
For 20 you will need 2 x 1-litre siphons, and for 75 you will need 7 x 1-litre siphons.

Start →

Pour the sugar into a wide saucepan and place over a low heat. As the sugar melts, you will see darker patches of caramel starting to appear. Stir to make an even, dark caramel colour.

Carefully pour in the cream and milk, and stir well.

Simmer the caramel gently for 5 minutes, whisking to make it smooth and even. Remove from the heat.

Put the egg yolks into large bowl and whisk lightly.

Gradually pour the caramel mixture onto the yolks, whisking continuously. Transfer the mixture to a clean saucepan.

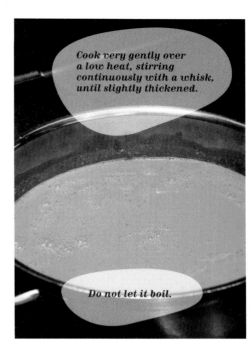

Cook very gently over a low heat, stirring continuously with a whisk, until slightly thickened.

Do not let it boil.

Pass the mixture through a fine-meshed sieve.

Insert the cartridge into the siphon, then fill with the caramel mixture.

Leave to cool in the fridge, or chill the siphon in a bucket of ice for 2 hours.

To serve the foam, first shake the siphon vigorously. Dispense the foam into bowls or glasses.

Add your choice of topping, such as toffee sauce or crushed toffees.

Cauliflower with béchamel

–

Pork ribs with barbecue sauce

–

Banana with lime

Cauliflower with béchamel

INGREDIENTS

BUY FRESH
* cauliflowers
* pork rib racks
* oranges
* bananas
* limes

IN THE CUPBOARD
* flour
* onions
* cloves
* dried bay leaves
* white peppercorns
* ground nutmeg
* extra-virgin olive oil
* salt
* barbecue sauce
* sugar

IN THE FRIDGE
* Parmesan cheese
* whole milk
* butter

Pork ribs
with
barbecue sauce

Banana
with
lime

	Hours before the meal
	4
	3½
	3
	2½
2 hours before Make the syrup for the bananas and cool	2
1½ hours before Roast the ribs in the oven	1½
1 hour before Slice the bananas and leave to marinate in the syrup Make the béchamel	1
30 minutes before Cut the cauliflower, then boil until just tender. Drain	½
5 minutes before Cover the cauliflower with the béchamel, then cook under the grill Cut the ribs and sprinkle with orange zest	
	Start of the meal
Just before dessert Spoon the bananas and some of their syrup into serving bowls	
	Dessert

Cauliflower with béchamel

If cooking this dish for 2 people, omit the onion and clove from the béchamel, and reduce the cooking time to 5–10 minutes.

	for 2	for 6	for 20	for 75
Whole milk	300 ml	900 ml	3 l	10 l
Butter	2 tsp	2 tbsp	100 g	375 g
Flour	2 tsp	2 tbsp	100 g	375 g
Small onions	-	1	1	1
Cloves	-	1	2	6
Dried bay leaves	¼	½	3	6
Freshly ground white pepper	1 pinch	2 pinches	0.3 g	1 g
Ground nutmeg	1 pinch	2 pinches	0.3 g	1 g
Cauliflowers	½	1½	4	15
Extra-virgin olive oil	10 ml	25 ml	80 ml	300 ml
Parmesan cheese, finely grated	40 g	120 g	400 g	1.5 kg

Start →

Pour the milk into a saucepan and bring to the boil. At the same time, melt the butter in another saucepan over a medium heat.

When the butter has melted, whisk in the flour. At first it will seem dry, but keep whisking until the mixture becomes smooth.

When the milk comes to a boil, gradually pour into the flour and butter, whisking continuously to ensure there are no lumps.

Insert the cloves into the onion and add it to the sauce with the bay leaf and nutmeg.

Leave the sauce to cook over a very low heat for 20 minutes, stirring frequently to prevent it from sticking.

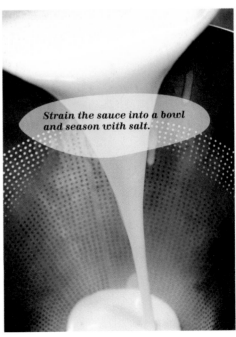

Strain the sauce into a bowl and season with salt.

Continue →

To prepare the cauliflower, cut off the stem and leaves.

Cut the head into florets no larger than 3 cm.

Bring a large pan of water to the boil. Add the cauliflower florets and cook for 8 minutes, or until just tender.

Drain the cauliflower, taking care not to damage the delicate florets.

Season with salt, white pepper and extra-virgin olive oil.

Spoon a layer of béchamel into a large heatproof baking dish and scatter the cauliflower over it, then cover with the rest of the sauce.

Heat the grill to high. Sprinkle the cauliflower with the grated Parmesan.

Cook under the grill for a couple of minutes until the cheese is golden and the sauce is bubbling around the edges.

Pork ribs
with
barbecue sauce

–

If you wish to make
your own barbecue sauce,
see the recipe on page 48.

	for 2	for 6	for 20	for 75
Pork rib racks, whole, weighing about 1.5 kg each	⅓ (6 ribs)	1	4	15
Salt	1 pinch	2 pinches	4 g	14 g
Barbecue sauce, either ready-made or home-made (see page 48)	100 g	300 g	1 kg	3.5 kg
Water	100 ml	300 ml	1 l	3.5 l
Oranges	½	1	2	4

Start →

Preheat the oven to 180°C/ 350°F/Gas Mark 4. Put the ribs into a roasting tin, meat side up, then season with salt.

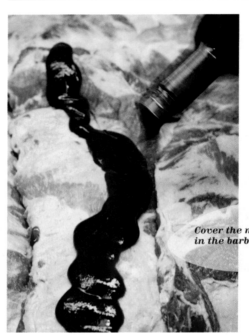

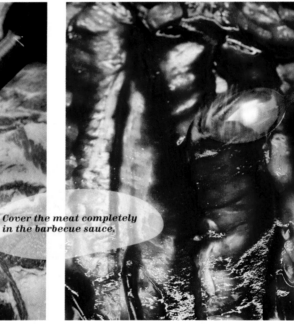

Cover the meat completely in the barbecue sauce.

Pour the water over the ribs to dilute the sauce a little.

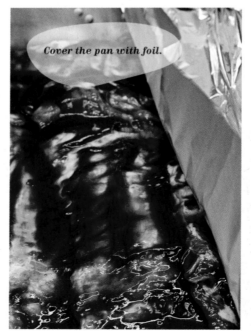

Cover the pan with foil.

Roast in the oven for 1½ hours.

Continue →

Baste with the barbecue sauce every 20 minutes to ensure the meat stays moist.

The racks are ready when they are dark, and golden, and the meat is falling away from the bone.

Once cooked, separate the ribs and place them in a serving dish.

Finish with a fine grating of orange zest to serve.

Banana with lime

This simple recipe is a good dessert to serve when few fresh fruits are in season.

•

For a special occasion you could add rum to the syrup: substitute 1 tsp, 30 ml, 100 ml or 375 ml of the water for rum for 2, 6, 20 or 75 people respectively.

•

You could also infuse a cinnamon stick or vanilla pod in the syrup while it cools.

	for 2	for 6	for 20	for 75
Sugar	2 tbsp	80 g	500 g	1.5 kg
Water	3 tbsp	150 ml	750 ml	2 l
Bananas	2	6	20	75
Limes	½	2	8	16

Start →

Pour the sugar and water into a medium-sized pan.

Heat gently until the sugar has dissolved. Pour the syrup into a shallow dish and leave to cool.

Finely grate the lime zest into the syrup.

Continue →

Squeeze the lime juice into the syrup and stir.

Peel, then thinly slice the bananas.

Put the banana slices into the syrup, then leave to marinate in the fridge for 1 hour before serving.

Serve in a small bowl with a couple of spoonfuls of syrup.

Gazpacho

–

Black rice with cuttlefish

–

Bread with chocolate & olive oil

INGREDIENTS

BUY FRESH
* small cucumbers
* red peppers
* ripe tomatoes
* white country-style
  loaf
* fresh cuttlefish,
  cleaned, with own ink
  (if possible)

IN THE CUPBOARD
* garlic
* onions
* extra-virgin olive oil
* olive oil
* sherry vinegar
* salt
* black pepper
* croutons
* paella rice
* dark chocolate,
  60% cocoa
* sea salt flakes

IN THE FRIDGE
* mayonnaise

IN THE FREEZER
* fish stock
  (see page 56)
* sofrito (see page 43)
* squid ink (optional,
  see page 272)
* picada (see page 41)

Gazpacho

Black rice with cuttlefish

Bread with chocolate & olive oil

ORGANIZING THE MENU	Hours before the meal
	4
	3½
	3
	2½
	2
	1½
	1
45 minutes before Make the gazpacho and chill in the fridge	½
25 minutes before Cut up the cuttlefish and heat the stock	
20 minutes before Start cooking the cuttlefish rice	
Grate the chocolate while the rice is cooking	
Just before eating Drizzle the gazpacho with oil and sprinkle with croutons	
	Start of the meal
Just before dessert Toast the bread and finish it with the chocolate, oil and salt	
	Dessert

Gazpacho

Gazpacho can be made ahead and frozen.
Defrost it in the fridge overnight.

•

Mayonnaise is an unusual
ingredient, but we like the creaminess
it adds to the soup.

•

For 2, you will need 4 tomatoes, 1 small
cucumber and 1 small red pepper.
For 6, you will need 12 tomatoes,
1 cucumber and 1 red pepper.

	for 2	for 6	for 20	for 75
Garlic cloves	1	3	50 g	150 g
Onions	1	2	120 g	400 g
Cucumber	20 g	60 g	200 g	800 g
Red pepper	25 g	75 g	300 g	1 kg
Ripe tomatoes	320 g	1 kg	3.2 kg	12 kg
500-g white country-style loaf (without crusts)	10 g	30 g	80 g	300 g
Water	4 tbsp	120 ml	400 ml	1.5 l
Olive oil, plus extra to serve	3 tbsp	6 tbsp	600 ml	2 l
Sherry vinegar	2 tsp	2 tbsp	5 tbsp	300 ml
Mayonnaise	2 tsp	1 tbsp	150 g	500 g
Croutons (see page 52)	40 g	120 g	400 g	1.5 kg

Start →

Peel and cut each garlic clove in half. Remove the green shoot inside, if there is one.

Fill a small saucepan with cold water and add the garlic.

Bring the water to the boil.

When the water begins to boil, lift the garlic out of the water and into a bowl of iced water to quickly cool it. Repeat this twice, always starting with cold water in the saucepan.

Peel the onion and cut in half, then cut into large chunks.

Peel the cucumber. Cut in half, then into large pieces.

Continue →

Halve the pepper, and remove the seeds and white membranes.

Chop the pepper, then set aside along with the cucumber and onion.

Cut the tomatoes into large wedges and put in a bowl with onions, cucumbers and peppers.

Add the bread, torn into pieces, then pour over the water.

Process everything together using a hand-held blender, or use a food processor.

Strain the gazpacho through a fine-meshed sieve.

Add the oil, vinegar and mayonnaise, then whisk or blend the soup until smooth and creamy.

Season with salt and pepper. Chill in the fridge before serving (at least 2 hours).

Serve the gazpacho in soup bowls with croutons, plus an extra drizzle of olive oil.

Black rice with cuttlefish

Ask your fishmonger to clean the cuttlefish for you, reserving the ink sacs and ink gland, which you use at the end of this recipe. If the cuttlefish is ready-cleaned without its ink, squid ink makes a great alternative. Buy in sachets.

•

A spoonful of aïoli (see page 53) makes an ideal accompaniment for this dish.

	for 2	for 6	for 20	for 75
Fresh cuttlefish, cleaned	200 g	600 g	2 kg	7 kg
Fish stock (see page 56)	600 ml	1.8 l	6 l	22 l
Olive oil	1½ tbsp	5 tbsp	200 ml	750 ml
Sofrito (see page 43)	1½ tbsp	80 g	300 g	1 kg
Paella rice	200 g	600 g	2 kg	7 kg
Squid ink (optional)	10 g	20 g	60 g	200 g
Picada (see page 41)	2 tsp	2 tbsp	120 g	400 g

Start →

If the cuttlefish has tentacles, pull them away from the body.

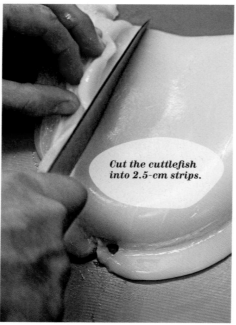

Cut the cuttlefish into 2.5-cm strips.

Then cut into 2.5-cm cubes.

Pour the fish stock into a saucepan, cover and bring to a simmer.

Put a large pan over a high heat and add the oil. Add the cuttlefish.

Fry for 2 minutes until golden in places.

Add the sofrito and continue to cook over a medium heat for 10 minutes. Add a teaspoon of water if the sofrito starts to stick on the bottom of the pan.

Continue →

Add the rice, stirring it into the cuttlefish. Fry for 10 minutes, stirring often.

Turn the heat to high and add a ladle of stock, stirring continuously. Once the stock has been absorbed, add another ladle and repeat until 5 minutes have passed.

Dissolve the squid or cuttlefish ink in a little of the remaining stock.

Add this to the rice, and then continue adding the rest of the stock.

Cook the rice for 12 more minutes, stirring frequently.

Add the picada and continue to cook for 2 minutes more, or until the rice has absorbed most of the liquid, and is just tender to the bite.

Season with salt, then serve.

Bread with chocolate & olive oil

–

Bread with chocolate is a popular dessert in Catalonia. When we cook it at elBulli we add extra-virgin olive oil and sea salt.

	for 2	for 6	for 20	for 75
500-g white country-style loaf, cut into 50-g slices	2 slices	6 slices	2 loaves	8 loaves
Dark chocolate, 60% cocoa	60 g	175 g	600 g	2 kg
Extra-virgin olive oil	1½ tbsp	4 tbsp	200 ml	750 ml
Sea salt flakes	1 pinch	½ tsp	2 tsp	40 g

Start →

Preheat the oven or grill to approximately 160°C/325°F/Gas Mark 3.

Coarsely grate the chocolate onto a plate.

Place the bread on a baking sheet or heatproof plate.

Peas & ham

–

Roast chicken with potato straws

–

Pineapple with molasses & lime

INGREDIENTS

BUY FRESH
* cured ham
* ham fat
* fresh mint
* whole chicken
* lemon
* pineapple
* lime

IN THE CUPBOARD
* olive oil
* cinnamon sticks
* onions
* dried bay leaves,
  rosemary and thyme
* black peppercorns
* garlic
* white wine
* salt
* potato straws
* molasses

IN THE FREEZER
* frozen peas
* ham stock (see
  page 59)

ORGANIZING THE MENU	Hours before the meal
	4
	3½
	3
	2½
	2
1 hour 30 minutes before Coat, stuff and roast the chicken	1½
1 hour before Turn the chicken over	1
30 minutes before Start cooking the peas Cut up the pineapple and arrange in a serving dish	½
10 minutes before Make the gravy Carve the chicken	
Just before eating Finish off the peas and serve Place the chicken on a serving dish and cover with the gravy	
	Start of the meal
Just before dessert Finish the pineapple with the lime zest, juice and molasses	
	Dessert

Peas & ham

You can use Serrano, Iberico, Bayonne, Parma or any other type of dry-cured ham for this recipe. If you cannot find ham fat, pancetta could be used instead.

•

The ham stock can be substituted with vegetable, chicken or meat stock (see page 59).

•

When they are in season, you could also make this with fresh peas, although they may be more expensive. Follow the recipe, but deduct 4 minutes from the cooking time.

	for 2	for 6	for 20	for 75
Olive oil	2 tsp	2 tbsp	3 tbsp	150 ml
Small onions, finely sliced	1	3	300 g	1 kg
Cured ham, thinly sliced	2	6	300 g	1 kg
Ham fat	10 g	25 g	120 g	425 g
Frozen peas	300 g	900 g	3 kg	10 kg
Cinnamon sticks	1	2	0.7 g	2.5 g
Sprigs fresh mint	1	3	25 g	85 g
Ham stock (see page 59)	5 tbsp	120 ml	400 ml	1.5 l

Start →

Heat the oil in a large frying pan, then add the onion and cook gently for 10 minutes until softened.

Cut the ham into thin, 3-cm long strips.

Chop the ham fat into very small pieces.

Add the chopped ham and fat to the onion.

Continue →

Fry gently for 2 minutes or until the fat has melted and the ham and onion are golden.

Stir in the frozen peas and continue to cook for 4 minutes.

Add the cinnamon and mint, then cover the pan and cook over a medium heat for 5 minutes.

Pour in the ham stock and simmer for 5 more minutes, covered, until the peas are very tender.

Turn off the heat and leave to stand, covered, for 5 minutes.

Remove one-tenth of the peas and process with a hand-held blender until creamy.

Add this back to the peas to make the sauce creamier.

Mix well.

Season to taste with salt and serve in soup plates.

Roast chicken with potato straws

The Catalan name for this dish is *pollo a l'ast*. It is a traditional dish of spit-roast chicken with lemon and herbs.

•

One chicken will serve four people. If you are cooking for two, the leftovers can be used in a salad the next day.

•

It is difficult to make the dried herb mixture in smaller quantities than those listed for 6–8, but the mixture will keep well in an airtight container.

	for 4	for 6–8	for 20	for 75
Dried bay leaves	–	3 g	10 g	25 g
Dried rosemary	–	40 g	100 g	325 g
Dried thyme	–	15 g	40 g	150 g
Black peppercorns	–	½ tsp	6 g	20 g
Chickens, whole, weighing 2 kg each	1	2	5	19
Olive oil	1 tbsp	2 tbsp	180 ml	650 ml
Lemons	1	2	5	19
Garlic cloves	2	4	40 g	150 g
White wine	2 tbsp	4 tbsp	60 ml	200 ml
Water	3 tbsp	6 tbsp	120 ml	450 ml
Salt	5 g	10 g	25 g	100 g
Potato straws	1 pack (about 100 g)	200 g	500 g	1.5 kg

Start →

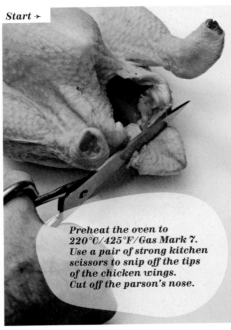

Preheat the oven to 220°C/425°F/Gas Mark 7. Use a pair of strong kitchen scissors to snip off the tips of the chicken wings. Cut off the parson's nose.

Put the chicken in a roasting tin, season inside and out with salt, then rub with oil. Finely grate lemon zest over the breast and legs.

Cut the lemon into pieces and place inside the chicken.

Put the bay, rosemary, thyme and peppercorns into a small food processor or blender and process to a fine powder.

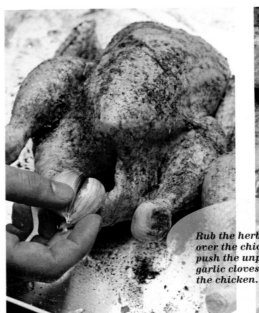

Rub the herb mixture over the chicken and push the unpeeled garlic cloves inside the chicken.

Continue →

Roast the chicken (breast facing down) for 25 minutes.

Turn the chicken over and roast for another 35 minutes, until golden and cooked through.

Remove the chicken and set aside to rest in a warm place. Return the roasting tin to the hob.

Pour in the wine and water, and loosen any sediment with a wooden spoon. Boil the cooking juices, bubbling them down to make a tasty gravy.

Carve the chicken into pieces and place on a serving dish.

Alternatively, serve the chicken whole.

Pour the gravy over and serve with potato straws.

Pineapple with molasses & lime

Substitute the molasses with honey or dark cane syrup, if you like.

•

For an easier preparation, simply top and tail the pineapple, quarter, remove the inner core, and serve in its skin.

•

To choose a ripe pineapple, look for one in which the central leaves can be pulled out easily.

	for 2	for 6	for 20	for 75
Pineapples	½	1	3	6
Limes	½	1½	3	8
Molasses	1½ tbsp	4 tbsp	225 g	800 g

Start →

Slice the top and bottom off the pineapple.

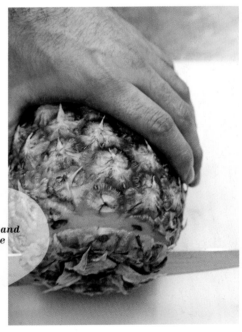

Cut away the skin and the first 5 mm of flesh.

Slice the pineapple in half lengthways.

Cut each half into four.

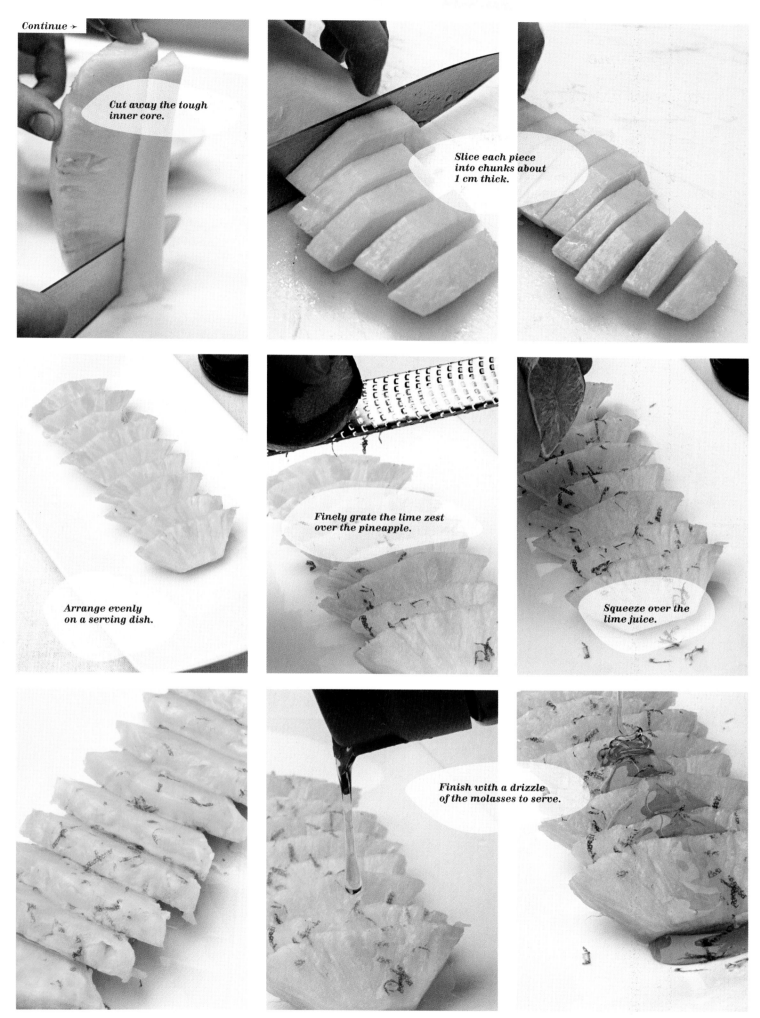

Cut away the tough inner core.

Slice each piece into chunks about 1 cm thick.

Arrange evenly on a serving dish.

Finely grate the lime zest over the pineapple.

Squeeze over the lime juice.

Finish with a drizzle of the molasses to serve.

Tagliatelle carbonara

–

Cod & green pepper sandwich

–

Almond soup with ice cream

INGREDIENTS

BUY FRESH
* long, mild green
  peppers
* fresh cod fillet
* white country-style
  loaf
* smoked streaky bacon

IN THE CUPBOARD
* sunflower oil
* flour
* salt
* olive oil
* egg tagliatelle
* whole blanched
  almonds
* sugar
* whole caramelized
  almonds

IN THE FRIDGE
* eggs
* mayonnaise
* Parmesan cheese
* whipping cream,
  35% fat

IN THE FREEZER
* ice cream

Cod & green pepper sandwich

Almond soup with ice cream

ORGANIZING THE MENU	Hours before the meal
The day before Chop, then soak the almonds in the water	4
	3½
	3
	2½
	2
	1½
	1
40 minutes before Make the almond soup and chill in the fridge	
35 minutes before Make the bacon cream for the carbonara	½
Cut the cod into pieces and get the flour, eggs and oil ready	
20 minutes before Fry the peppers	
Just before eating Fry the cod, toast the bread and assemble the sandwich	
Boil the pasta while you eat the sandwich	Start of the meal
Finish the pasta and serve with grated Parmesan	
Just before dessert Scoop or quenelle the ice cream	
	Dessert

Tagliatelle carbonara

For small quantities you can increase the amount of egg yolks for a richer flavour.

	for 2	for 6	for 20	for 75
Smoked streaky bacon	120 g	360 g	1.2 kg	4 kg
Olive oil	1½ tbsp	6 tbsp	300 ml	1 l
Whipping cream, 35% fat	200 ml	600 ml	2.2 l	9 l
Water	600 ml	1.8 l	6 l	22 l
Salt	1 tsp	1 tbsp	30 g	110 g
Egg tagliatelle	200 g	600 g	2 kg	7.5 kg
Egg yolks	2	6	150 g	500 g
Parmesan cheese, finely grated	40 g	150 g	500 g	2 kg

Start →

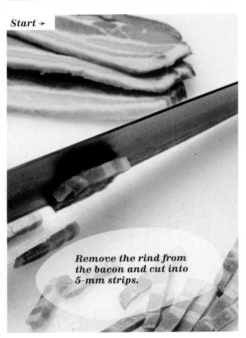

Remove the rind from the bacon and cut into 5-mm strips.

Place a large saucepan over a low heat, add the oil and then the bacon.

Fry gently for 10 minutes until the bacon has browned.

Set aside one-eighth of the cream, then add the rest to the bacon.

Simmer for 20 minutes.

Continue →

Season with salt and pepper before removing from the heat.

Bring the water to the boil, add the salt and pasta.

Cook for 7 minutes, or until the pasta is tender but still firm to the bite (check the instructions on the packet).

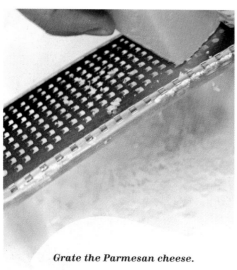

Grate the Parmesan cheese.

Whisk together the egg yolks and the reserved cream.

Drain the pasta, then return to the pan.

Add the bacon cream to the pasta.

Stirring constantly, add the egg yolk and cream mix. The eggs will thicken slightly as they come into contact with the hot pasta.

Serve with the grated Parmesan.

Cod & green pepper sandwich

In Spain this dish is known as a *montadito*, which is a traditional dish consisting of various cooked ingredients on a slice of toasted country bread.

•

Ask your fishmonger to clean, gut and fillet the fish for you if you prefer. Any white fish, such as hake or monkfish, can be used instead of cod.

•

When frying in large quantities, use a large saucepan, and never fill the pan more than half full with oil.

	for 2	for 6	for 20	for 75
Sunflower oil	150 ml	500 ml	1.5 l	5 l
Long, mild green peppers	2	6	20	75
Fresh cod fillet, skin on and scaled	300 g	1.5 kg	5 kg	16 kg
Salt	1 pinch	½ tsp	8 g	30 g
Flour	1½ tbsp	90 g	300 g	1 kg
Eggs	1	2	4	10
500-g white country-style loaf, cut into 50-g slices	2 slices	6 slices	2 loaves	6 loaves
Mayonnaise	2 tbsp	90 g	300 g	1 kg

Start →

Pour a little of the oil into a frying pan and add the peppers.

Fry until they are soft and well browned on both sides.

Season with a little salt to taste, then lift the peppers onto kitchen paper to absorb the excess oil.

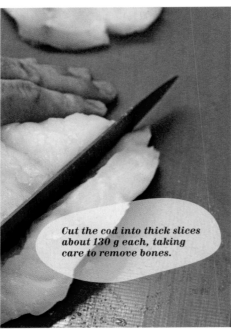

Cut the cod into thick slices about 130 g each, taking care to remove bones.

Season the fish with the salt.

Put the flour onto a plate and use to coat the fish. Heat the remaining oil in a pan.

Continue →

Pat the excess flour off the fish.

Beat the egg, then dip a piece of the floured cod into it. Let the excess drip away.

Repeat with all the pieces.

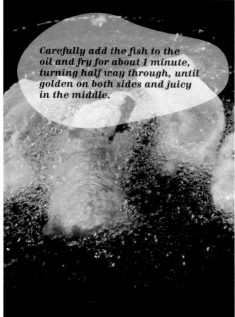

Carefully add the fish to the oil and fry for about 1 minute, turning half way through, until golden on both sides and juicy in the middle.

Lift the fried cod from the pan with a slotted spoon and drain on kitchen paper. Preheat the grill or oven to high.

Spread the bread over a baking sheet.

Toast the bread under the grill or in the oven until golden on both sides.

To assemble the sandwich, top the toast with a green pepper followed by a piece of fried cod.

Serve with the mayonnaise.

Almond soup with ice cream

We do not recommend making any less than the quantity given for 6 people. Any leftover soup will keep well in the fridge.

•

Caramel, toffee or nut-flavoured ice cream could be substituted for the nougat ice cream, and any other caramelized nut could be substituted for the almonds.

•

Marcona almonds are a Spanish, sweet-flavoured variety. Any good-quality almond can be used.

	for 2	for 6	for 20	for 75
Whole blanched Marcona almonds	-	240 g	600 g	3 kg
Water	-	600 ml	1.5 l	8 l
Sugar	-	80 g	175 g	700 g
Whole caramelized almonds	-	18 g	150 g	500 g
Nougat ice cream	-	180 g	600 g	2 kg

Start →

Put the almonds into a food processor and roughly chop.

Tip them into a large bowl, then add the water.

Leave to soak for 12 hours or overnight in the fridge.

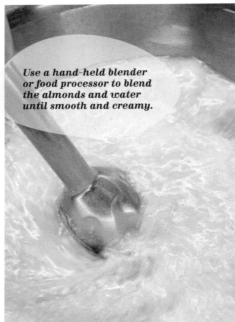

Use a hand-held blender or food processor to blend the almonds and water until smooth and creamy.

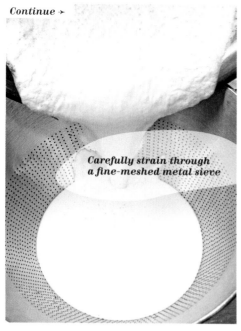

Continue →

Carefully strain through a fine-meshed metal sieve

Use the back of a ladle to help the soup pass through the sieve.

Add the sugar and whisk until it dissolves.

To serve, put a triangle of three caramelized almonds in the bottom of a bowl. Place a scoop of nougat ice cream in the centre of the triangle.

Pour the almond soup around the ice cream.

Chickpeas with spinach & egg

–

Glazed teriyaki pork belly

–

Sweet potato with honey & cream

INGREDIENTS

BUY FRESH
* ripe tomatoes
* belly pork
* sweet potatoes

IN THE CUPBOARD
* olive oil
* garlic
* ground cumin
* cooked chickpeas
* salt
* black peppercorns
* cornflour
* medium onions
* teriyaki sauce
* sugar
* runny honey

IN THE FRIDGE
* eggs
* whipping cream,
  35% fat

IN THE FREEZER
* whole-leaf spinach
* chicken stock (see
  page 57)

ORGANIZING THE MENU

	Hours before the meal
	4
	3½
	3
	2½
2 hours before Simmer the belly pork for 1½ hours	2
Blend and drain the tomatoes and chop the garlic for the chickpeas	1½
	1
45 minutes before Bake the sweet potatoes	
30 minutes before Cut the belly pork and cover with teriyaki sauce. Roast for 30 minutes, basting once	½
Chop, boil and drain the spinach, then finish the chickpea recipe	
Just before eating Boil or poach the eggs	
Whip the cream to soft peaks and set aside in the fridge	
	Start of the meal
Just before dessert Split the sweet potatoes and spread with the honey	
	Dessert

Chickpeas with spinach & egg

This dish is good topped with either a boiled or poached egg, or we sometimes cook the egg in its shell in a low-temperature water bath called a Roner. This gives a very soft and silky result. To boil, as well as poach an egg, see page 19.

•

To substitute fresh, raw spinach for frozen spinach, allow 100 g for 2 people, 270 g for 6, 800 g for 20 and 3.25 kg for 75. The cooking time will be slightly longer.

	for 2	for 6	for 20	for 75
Frozen whole leaf spinach, defrosted	65 g	200 g	600 g	2.5 kg
Ripe tomatoes	2	5	1.2 kg	4 kg
Olive oil	2 tbsp	6 tbsp	300 ml	1 kg
Garlic cloves	2	6	40 g	120 g
Ground cumin	1 pinch	2 pinches	1 g	5 g
Cooked chickpeas, drained	320 g	1 kg	3.2 kg	12 kg
Chicken stock (see page 57)	200 ml	600 ml	2 l	7 l
Cornflour	1 tsp	3 tsp	1 tbsp	50 g
Eggs	2	6	20	75

For 2 you will need 2 tomatoes, and for 6 you will need 5 tomatoes.

Start →

Bring a medium pan of water to the boil. Cut the spinach into 3-cm pieces and boil for 1 minute.

Drain the spinach and set aside.

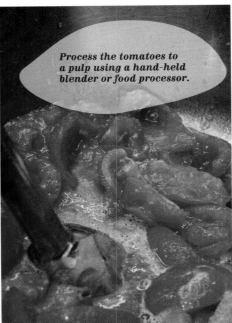

Process the tomatoes to a pulp using a hand-held blender or food processor.

Set a fine-meshed sieve over a pan. Pour the tomatoes into the sieve and leave to drain for 15 minutes without pressing.

Continue →

Meanwhile, finely chop the garlic.

Heat the oil over a medium heat in a large pan, then add the garlic and the tomato pulp.

Add the chickpeas and cumin, and cook for 30 seconds.

Add the stock and bring to the boil.

Meanwhile, cook the eggs to your liking (see note.)

Stir in the spinach and season with salt and pepper.

Mix the cornflour with a little cold water until smooth, then add to the chickpeas and spinach. Stir until slightly thickened.

Spoon the chickpeas into serving dishes, and top with the eggs.

Glazed teriyaki pork belly

Teriyaki is a sweet Japanese sauce used for marinating before roasting or grilling.

•

You can make the teriyaki sauce yourself (see page 50), or use a good-quality shop-bought sauce.

	for 2	for 6	for 20	for 75
Pork belly	400 g	1.2 kg	4 kg	15 kg
Water	1 l	2.5 l	10 l	40 l
Salt	2 pinches	2 tsp	30 g	100 g
Black peppercorns	4	12	4 g	15 g
Garlic cloves	1	3	25 g	85 g
Onions, roughly chopped	¼	1	130 g	450 g
Teriyaki sauce (see page 50)	200 g	600 g	2 kg	7.5 kg

Start →

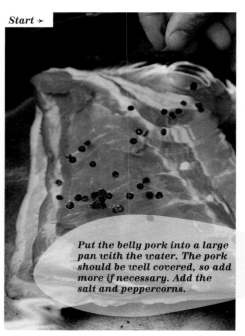

Put the belly pork into a large pan with the water. The pork should be well covered, so add more if necessary. Add the salt and peppercorns.

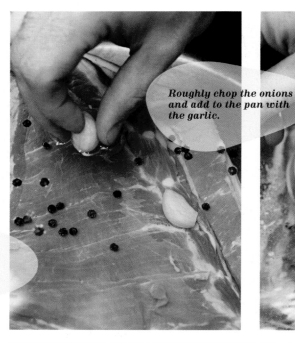

Roughly chop the onions and add to the pan with the garlic.

Bring the water to a simmer.

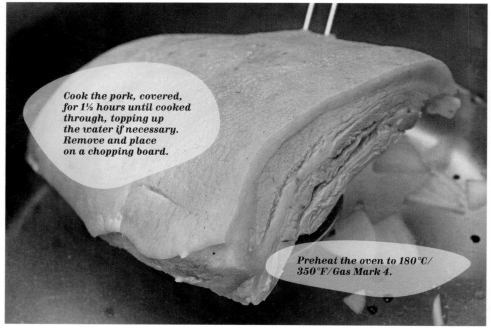

Cook the pork, covered, for 1½ hours until cooked through, topping up the water if necessary. Remove and place on a chopping board.

Preheat the oven to 180°C/350°F/Gas Mark 4.

Continue ➜

Cut the belly pork into strips about 2 cm thick.

Place the pork in a roasting tin in a single layer, then cover with the teriyaki sauce.

Roast the pork for 30 minutes, regularly basting with the teriyaki sauce to glaze.

Serve the pork with spoonfuls of the teriyaki sauce.

Sweet potato with honey & cream

The sweet potato is native to central and South America, where it is used in both sweet and savoury dishes. This simple recipe shows how well it works as a dessert.

	for 2	for 6	for 20	for 75
Sweet potatoes, 100 g each	2	6	20	75
Whipping cream, 35% fat	4 tbsp	180 g	600 g	2 kg
Sugar	1½ tsp	5 tsp	80 g	300 g
Honey	2 tbsp	6 tbsp	300 g	1 kg

Start →

Preheat the oven to 180°C/350°F/Gas Mark 4.

Put the sweet potatoes into a roasting tin and roast for 40 minutes.

When the sweet potatoes are almost cooked, pour the cream into a large bowl.

Add the sugar.

Use a whisk or free-standing mixer to whip the cream to soft peaks.

Remove the sweet potatoes from the oven. They will be crisp on the outside and tender in the middle.

Cut them in half lengthwise.

Put the sweet potatoes cut-side up on a serving plate, then pour over the honey.

Serve the hot sweet potatoes with the whipped cream.

Potatoes & green beans with Chantilly

–

Quails with couscous

–

Caramelized pears

**Potatoes &
green beans
with Chantilly**

**Quails
with couscous**

INGREDIENTS

BUY FRESH
* green flat beans
* lemons
* quails
* spinach
* fresh mint
* Conference pears
* fruit sorbet
  or ice cream
* ras el hanout

IN THE CUPBOARD
* potatoes
* salt
* N₂O cartridges
* black peppercorns
* honey
* extra-virgin olive oil
* pine nuts
* raisins
* couscous
* sugar

IN THE FRIDGE
* mayonnaise
* butter
* whipping cream,
  35% fat

IN THE FREEZER
* chicken stock
  (see page 57)

Caramelized pears

ORGANIZING THE MENU	Hours before the meal
	4
	3½
	3
	2½
	2
1½ hours before	1½
Prepare the quails and chill in the fridge	
Make the caramelized pears and leave to cool at room temperature	
	1
45 minutes before	
Cut up the potatoes and trim the beans	
30 minutes before	½
Boil the potatoes	
Make the Chantilly foam, fill the siphon and chill	
Start grilling the quails	
Heat the stock. Toast the pine nuts and add the raisins and couscous	
10 minutes before	
Add the spinach, stock and ras el hanout to the couscous. Cover and set aside	
Boil the beans, then drain	
	Start of the meal
Just before main course	
Finish with the lemon zest and juice	
	Main course

Potatoes & green beans with Chantilly

Perona beans are a variety of green beans commonly grown in Spain. Runner beans or other flat green beans would also work.

•

If you do not have a siphon, you can whip the cream into soft peaks and fold it through the mayonnaise instead, but of course the texture will not be quite the same.

	for 2	for 6	for 20	for 75
Medium potatoes	2	1.2 kg	4 kg	16 kg
Green Perona beans	240 g	720 g	2.4 kg	9 kg
For the Chantilly foam:				
Whipping cream, 35% fat	125 ml	125 ml	420 g	1.25 kg
Mayonnaise	150 g	300 g	500 g	1.5 kg
Lemon juice	1 tsp	1 tsp	140 ml	360 ml
N_2O cartridges for the siphon	2	2	4	10

Start →

Fill a large pan with salted water and bring to the boil. Cut the potatoes into pieces roughly 3 cm across.

Boil the potatoes in the salted water for 25 minutes, or until tender.

While the potatoes are cooking, whisk together the mayonnaise and cream in a large bowl.

Squeeze the lemon juice, strain through a sieve, then add to the bowl. Whisk until evenly combined. Season with salt.

Continue →

Put the mixture into the siphon and close the top.

Charge the siphon with the cartridge, then chill in the fridge until later.

Bring another pan of salted water to the boil.

Trim the tips of the beans, then cut the beans into finger-length pieces.

Boil the green beans for 4 minutes, or until just tender.

Drain the potatoes and beans.

Serve the potatoes in a bowl, topped with the beans. Dispense the Chantilly foam on top of the beans, or in a separate dish to the side.

Quail with couscous

When cooking for 20 or 75, we recommend serving one quail per person. Poussins or chicken breasts can be substituted for the quail. For this dish, we split each quail down the middle, which helps the meat to cook quickly and evenly. If you prefer not to prepare the quail yourself, ask your butcher to do it.

•

Ras el hanout is a classic spice mixture used in Moroccan cuisine.

	for 2	for 6	for 20	for 75
Quails	4	12	20	75
Ras el hanout	1½ tsp	3½ tsp	28 g	90 g
Sprigs fresh mint	4	12	1 bunch	2 bunches
Runny honey	2 tsp	1½ tbsp	150 g	400 g
Extra-virgin olive oil	2 tsp	1½ tbsp	100 ml	300 ml
Lemons	½	1	2	6
Chicken stock	100 ml	300 ml	1.3 l	4 l
Extra-virgin olive oil	1½ tbsp	4 tbsp	125 ml	370 ml
Pine nuts	2 tsp	2 tbsp	190 g	560 g
Raisins	2 tsp	2 tbsp	160 g	480 g
Couscous	75 g	225 g	1 kg	3 kg
Spinach	20 g	60 g	250 g	800 g

Start →

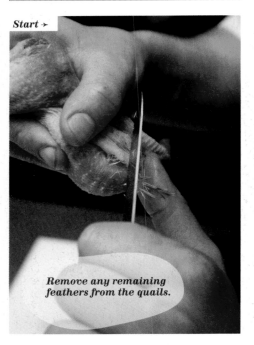

Remove any remaining feathers from the quails.

Use strong kitchen scissors or poultry shears to cut off the wing tips.

Use the scissors or shears to cut right through the back of each quail.

Open out the quails, then clean the insides, rinse with cold water and pat dry with kitchen paper.

Put the quails into a roasting tin, season with salt, pepper and two-thirds of the ras el hanout. Chill for 1 hour.

Pour the chicken stock into a saucepan and bring to the boil. Heat the grill to medium.

Pick the mint leaves from the stems and shred finely.

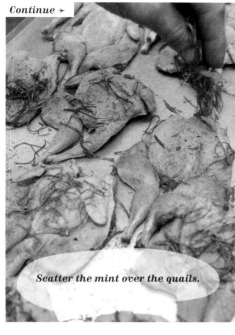

Scatter the mint over the quails.

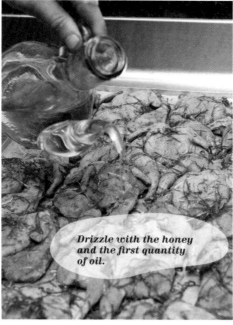

Drizzle with the honey and the first quantity of oil.

Grill the quails for 4 minutes, turning from time to time, until golden and juicy. Keep them warm under the kitchen foil.

Meanwhile, heat the second quantity of oil in a wide pan, then add the pine nuts. Cook over a low heat for 5 minutes, stirring often, until golden.

Add the raisins to the pine nuts and stir for 30 seconds. Add the couscous and cook for 1 minute.

Add the spinach and remaining ras el hanout and pour in the chicken stock. Cover the pan, remove from the heat and leave the couscous to absorb the stock.

Stir the couscous to separate the grains.

Spoon the couscous onto a serving dish, then top with the quails. Finish with the finely grated zest and the juice of the lemon.

Caramelized pears

These are delicious served with fruit sorbet, or vanilla or chocolate ice cream.

•

It is best to choose pears that have just ripened.

	for 2	for 6	for 20	for 75
Conference pears	1	3	10	38
Sugar	1½ tbsp	3½ tbsp	350 g	1.12 kg
Butter	2 tbsp	2 tbsp	200 g	600 g
Hot water	200 ml	600 ml	500 ml	1.5 l
Ice cream or sorbet	100 g	300 g	1.2 kg	3.5 kg
Sprigs fresh mint	1	3	10	38

Start →

Peel the pears.

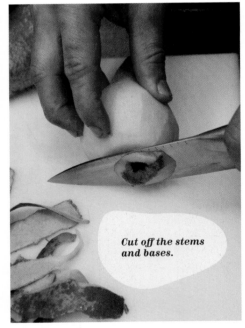

Cut off the stems and bases.

Use an apple corer to remove the cores.

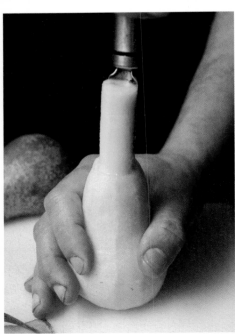

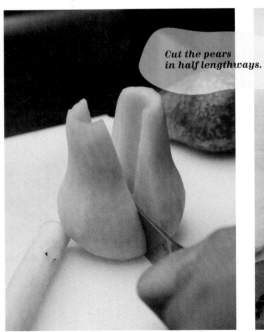

Cut the pears in half lengthways.

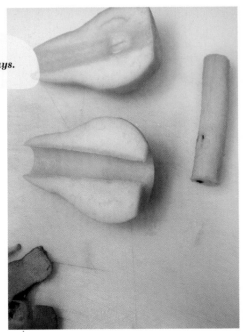

Continue →

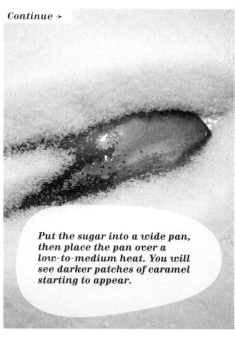

Put the sugar into a wide pan, then place the pan over a low-to-medium heat. You will see darker patches of caramel starting to appear.

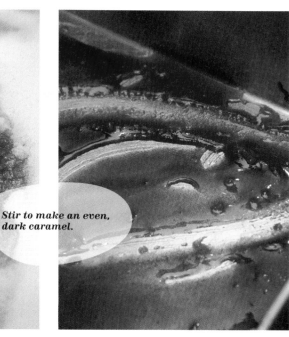

Stir to make an even, dark caramel.

Add the butter to the caramel, then stir until melted and even.

Carefully add the pears to the pan, core-side down.

Pour in the hot water. The caramel will bubble dramatically, so take care not to burn yourself.

Cook the pears for 5 minutes, turning after 2½ minutes.

The pears will be soft and the caramel sauce silky. Remove from the heat and leave to cool at room temperature.

Serve the pears and caramel sauce with ice cream or sorbet. Decorate with a few mint leaves.

Fish soup

–

Sausages with mushrooms

–

Oranges with honey, olive oil & salt

INGREDIENTS

BUY FRESH
* whole, fresh, cleaned fish from the market
* baguette (or use day-old bread)
* butifarra sausages, or other good-quality coarse pork sausages
* fresh rosemary
* fresh thyme
* medium white mushrooms
* fresh parsley
* large oranges

IN THE CUPBOARD
* garlic
* extra-virgin olive oil
* olive oil
* mild paprika
* pastis, or any anise-based liqueur
* *vino rancio* or dry sherry
* salt
* black peppercorns
* honey-flavoured boiled sweets
* runny honey
* sea salt flakes

IN THE FREEZER
* sofrito (see page 43)
* picada (see page 41)

Fish soup

Sausages with mushrooms

ORGANIZING THE MENU	Hours before the meal
	4
	3½
	3
	2½
	2
	1½
1 hour (or up to 2 days) before Make the soup	1
30 minutes before Pinch the sausage meat into balls and fry for a few minutes	½
Slice the mushrooms	
Peel and slice the oranges, then set aside in the fridge	
Crush the sweets	
20 minutes before Fry the mushrooms and finish cooking the sausages with the herbs and seasoning	
5 minutes before Reheat the soup	
Put the sausages and mushrooms in a dish and keep warm	
	Start of the meal
Just before dessert Dress the oranges with the honey, olive oil, crushed sweets and salt flakes	
	Dessert

Fish soup

Any anise-based liqueur
can be used instead of pastis,
or you could add a little chopped fennel
to the pan just before serving.

•

Choose an economical mixture of fish,
crabs and crustaceans and use the whole
fish to give a rich, deep flavour. Ask
the fishmonger to clean and gut
the fish for you if you prefer.

•

This soup is good served with
croutons (see page 52).

	for 2	for 6	for 20	for 75
Garlic cloves	3	9	25 g	90 g
Olive oil	2 tbsp	6 tbsp	180 ml	650 ml
Sofrito (see page 43)	1½ tbsp	4 tbsp	240 g	800 g
Mix of fresh whole fish, ready-cleaned	300 g	900 g	3 kg	10 kg
Sweet paprika	2 tsp	2 tbsp	25 g	90 g
Water	700 ml	2 l	5 l	16 l
Bread (day-old is good)	20 g	60 g	120g	400 g
Picada (see page 41)	2 tsp	2 tbsp	120 g	400 g
Pastis	1 dash	2 dashes	1 tsp	1½ tbsp

Start →

Roughly crush the garlic cloves with the back of a knife or a pestle.

Heat half the oil in a large pan and fry the garlic gently for a few minutes until golden.

Add the sofrito and fry gently for 10 minutes, stirring frequently.

Leave any small fish whole. For larger fish, use sharp scissor or a sharp knife to cut them into rough large pieces.

Add them to the pan.

Sprinkle in the paprika, then add the water.

Continue →

Cook the soup for 20 minutes at a gentle simmer.

While the soup cooks, fry the bread slices in a frying pan with the remaining oil until deep golden.

Strain the soup into another large saucepan.

Add the fried bread and the picada to the pan, then cook for another 10 minutes.

Process the soup with a hand-held blender until smooth. You could also use a jug blender.

Season with salt.

Pour in the pastis or anise-flavoured liqueur.

Serve with croutons, if you like.

Sausages with mushrooms

Butifarra are traditional sausages from Catalonia. The original Catalan name for this dish is *butifarra esparracada*, which literally means 'butifarra sausage broken into little pieces'. Any good-quality pork sausage can be substituted.

•

You could use wild mushrooms instead of white mushrooms, and parsley oil could be substituted for the fresh parsley.

•

Vino rancio is a Catalan fortified oxidized wine. If you cannot find it, use dry sherry instead.

	for 2	for 6	for 20	for 75
Butifarra, or other good-quality coarse pork sausages	250 g	750 g	2.5 kg	9.5 kg
Olive oil	3 tbsp	6 tbsp	600 ml	2 l
Garlic cloves	4	12	60 g	200 g
Sprigs fresh rosemary	1	1	3 g	10 g
Sprigs fresh thyme	1	1	3 g	10 g
Medium white mushrooms	200 g	600 g	1.8 kg	6.5 kg
Vino rancio or dry sherry	3 tbsp	120 ml	200 ml	750 ml
Fresh parsley, chopped	1 tsp	1 tbsp	175 g	600 g

Start →

Remove the skins from the sausages and pinch the sausage meat into walnut-size balls.

Heat the oil in a large frying pan. Gently fry the sausages for 3–4 minutes over a medium-high heat, until golden on all sides.

Peel and lightly crush the garlic cloves. Add to the pan along with the sprigs of rosemary and thyme.

Continue to fry for 5 minutes.

Continue →

Meanwhile, clean, trim and quarter the mushrooms.

Pour the vino rancio into the pan and scrape the bottom to loosen any sediment. Use a little water if needed. Remove the pan from the heat.

In another pan, fry the mushrooms in a little oil for 5 minutes until golden.

Add the mushrooms to the sausages and cook for 15 minutes over a medium heat until they are cooked through.

Pick the leaves from the parsley stalks and finely chop.

Stir in the chopped parsley, season with salt and pepper, and serve.

Oranges with honey, olive oil & salt

You can use coarse salt instead of salt flakes (although the texture will be more crunchy.)

	for 2	for 6	for 20	for 75
Honey-flavoured boiled sweets	3	9	65 g	250 g
Large oranges	2	6	20	75
Runny honey	1½ tbsp	4 tbsp	150 g	500 g
Extra-virgin olive oil	2 tbsp	6 tbsp	150 ml	500 ml
Sea salt flakes	1 pinch	1 generous pinch	1 tsp	1 tbsp

Start →

Place the sweets between two sheets of baking parchment and crush into small pieces with a rolling pin or other heavy utensil.

Using a sharp knife, cut the ends off the oranges.

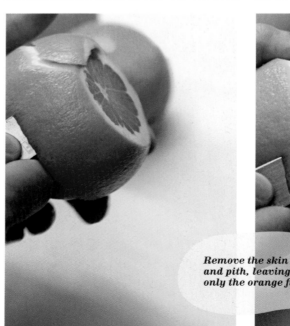

Remove the skin and pith, leaving only the orange flesh.

Continue →

Cut the oranges into slices about 5 mm thick, then spread them out in a single layer in a serving dish.

Pour the honey over the oranges.

Drizzle with the olive oil.

Sprinkle with the sea salt flakes.

Scatter with the crushed sweets, and serve.

Mussels with paprika

–

Baked sea bass

–

Caramel pudding

Mussels with paprika

INGREDIENTS

BUY FRESH
* medium mussels
* fresh parsley
* whole sea bass
* ripe tomatoes
* fresh thyme
* fresh rosemary
* potatoes

IN THE CUPBOARD
* onions
* garlic
* olive oil
* mild paprika
* flour
* salt
* black peppercorns
* sugar
* white rum

IN THE FRIDGE
* eggs
* whipping cream,
  35% fat

ORGANIZING THE MENU	Hours before the meal
	4
	3½
	3
	2½
	2
	1½
1 hour before Prepare and steam the caramel puddings	1
Prepare all the ingredients for the fish	
45 minutes before Bake the potato, onion and tomato for the fish	
Clean the mussels and prepare the sauce	½
15 minutes before Add the sea bass to the vegetables and put in the oven	
Just before eating Add the mussels to the sauce	
	Start of the meal
Drizzle the baked sea bass with olive oil	
	Main course
Just before dessert Whip the rum cream to soft peaks	
	Dessert

Mussels with paprika

It is essential to cook the mussels at the last minute so that they do not become tough.

•

Any mussels that do not open should be discarded.

	for 2	for 6	for 20	for 75
Mussels	600 g	1.4 kg	6 kg	18 kg
Garlic cloves	1	3	80 g	200 g
Olive oil	1½ tbsp	4 tbsp	400 g	1.2 kg
Mild paprika	½ tsp	1 tsp	18 g	45 g
Flour	1 tsp	3 tsp	150 g	500 g
Water	200 ml	450 ml	1.2 l	4 l
Fresh parsley, finely chopped	2 tsp	1½ tbsp	1 bunch	3 bunches

Start →

Scrub and de-beard the mussels under cold running water.

Finely chop the garlic.

Heat the oil in a saucepan, then add the garlic. Cook for 1 minute.

Add the paprika and cook for a couple of seconds.

Continue →

Stir in the flour.

Mix well.

Pour in the water, stirring to make a smooth sauce.

Boil for 10 minutes, or until the sauce is thickened and tasty.

Finely chop the parsley. Add half the parsley to the sauce.

Add the cleaned mussels and cover the pan.

Cook for 5 minutes.

The mussels are ready when they have opened up completely. Discard any that have stayed shut.

Remove the pan from the heat.

Sprinkle with the rest of the parsley and serve. Season with salt.

Baked sea bass

Ask your fishmonger to clean and gut the fish for you if you prefer.

•

This dish can be made with other varieties of fish, such as bream.

	for 2	for 6	for 20	for 75
Sea bass, 300 g each	2	6	20	75
Medium potatoes	2	6	3 kg	14 kg
Ripe tomatoes	2	6	1.5 kg	5.2 kg
Medium onions	1	3	1.1 kg	3.4 kg
Garlic cloves	3	9	200 g	600 g
Sprigs fresh thyme	2	6	20	75
Sprigs fresh rosemary	2	6	20	75
Olive oil	2 tbsp	6 tbsp	400 ml	1.2 l

Start →

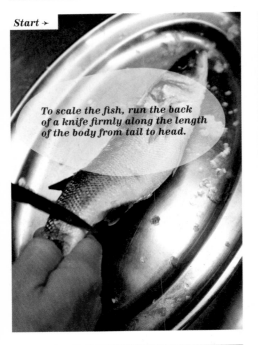

To scale the fish, run the back of a knife firmly along the length of the body from tail to head.

Cut the fins away from the body using kitchen scissors.

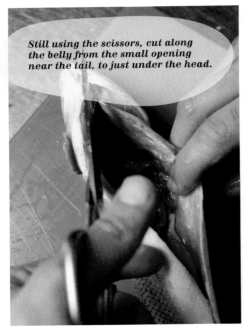

Still using the scissors, cut along the belly from the small opening near the tail, to just under the head.

Remove the insides using your hands or a spoon, then rinse under cold water to remove any blood.

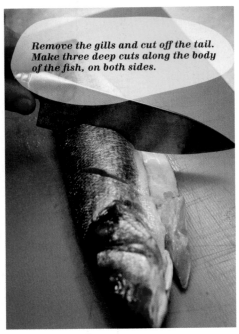

Remove the gills and cut off the tail. Make three deep cuts along the body of the fish, on both sides.

Preheat the oven to 180°C/ 350°F/Gas Mark 4.

Peel the potatoes and cut into slices about 1 cm thick.

Continue →

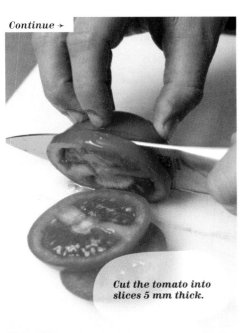

Cut the tomato into slices 5 mm thick.

Thinly slice the onion.

Roughly crush the whole garlic cloves, leaving the skins on.

Pour a little oil into a large roasting tin. Spread half of the potato in the tin, then half of the tomato and half of the onion.

Season with salt and pepper. Repeat the layers of potato, tomato and onion.

Scatter with the garlic and herbs. Pour over most of the remaining oil. Cover the tin with foil, then bake in the oven for 30 minutes.

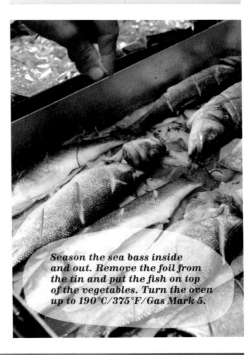

Season the sea bass inside and out. Remove the foil from the tin and put the fish on top of the vegetables. Turn the oven up to 190°C/375°F/Gas Mark 5.

Return the tin to the oven, uncovered, for 12 minutes, or until the fish is opaque and flakes easily from the back bone.

Finish with a little more olive oil and a few sprigs of rosemary and thyme.

Caramel pudding

Depending on the size of your heatproof moulds, you may need to allow longer for the puddings to steam.

•

The puddings are ready when they have a consistent texture, and when a knife inserted comes out clean.

	for 2	for 6	for 20	for 75
Sugar	92 g	275 g	920 g	2.76 kg
Water	50 ml	150 ml	500 ml	1.5 l
Egg yolks	4	12	40	120
Whipping cream, 35% fat	1 tsp	1½ tbsp	100 ml	300 ml
For the rum cream:				
Whipping cream, 35% fat	1½ tbsp	100 ml	500 ml	1.5 l
White rum	½ tsp	2 tsp	100 ml	300 ml

Start →

Mix the sugar and water in a saucepan. Place the pan over a low heat and let the sugar dissolve without the water boiling.

When the sugar has dissolved, boil the syrup until it reaches 109°C (228°F) on a sugar thermometer.

Put the egg yolks in a large bowl, then beat together with a balloon whisk.

Strain the mixture through a fine-meshed sieve.

Pour the syrup into the eggs a little at a time, stirring continuously with a spatula to avoid making any bubbles.

Continue →

Pour in the cream.

Stir in until evenly combined.

Pour into coffee cups, small glasses or similar heatproof moulds and cover with cling film.

Place the cups or glasses in a steamer basket over a pan of boiling water. Cover and steam for 10 minutes.

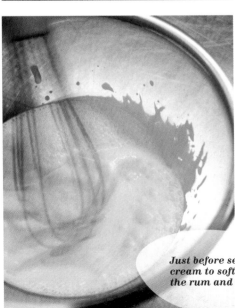

Just before serving, whip the cream to soft peaks, then add the rum and whip again.

Serve the puddings at room temperature.

–

Meal 28

–

Melon with cured ham

–

Rice with duck

–

Chocolate cake

INGREDIENTS

BUY FRESH
* large ripe melon
* cured ham
* duck legs

IN THE CUPBOARD
* olive oil
* salt
* white wine
* paella rice
* black peppercorns
* dark chocolate,
  60% cocoa
* sugar

IN THE FRIDGE
* butter
* eggs

IN THE FREEZER
* chicken stock
  (see page 57)
* sofrito (see page 43)
* picada (see page 41)

**Rice
with duck**

**Chocolate
cake**

ORGANIZING THE MENU

	Hours before the meal
	4
	3½
	3
	2½
	2
	1½
1 hour before Make the cake mixture and pipe into the moulds	1
40 minutes before Boil the stock and cut up the duck, ready for the rice	
30 minutes before Start frying the duck	½
Bake the chocolate cakes	
20 minutes before Add the stock to the rice	
Just before eating Cut up the melon	
	Start of the meal
Just before dessert Remove the cakes from the moulds and serve with warm chocolate	
	Dessert

Melon with cured ham

The ham should be served at room temperature alongside the melon. Do not place slices of ham over the melon, or they will become soggy.

•

You can also serve this dish as a dessert.

•

The best melon varieties to choose are cantaloupe or *piel de sapo* (toad skin).

	for 2	for 6	for 20	for 75
Large ripe melon	¼	1	3	10
Cured ham, thinly sliced	100 g	250 g	600 g	2.25 kg

Start →

Cut the melon in half, then trim off the ends

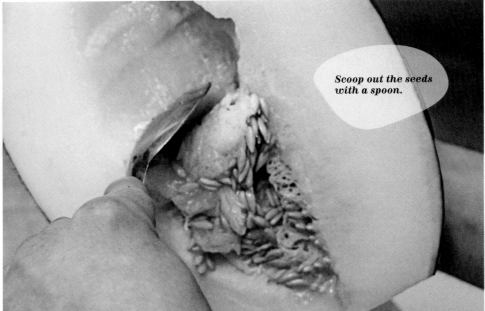

Scoop out the seeds with a spoon.

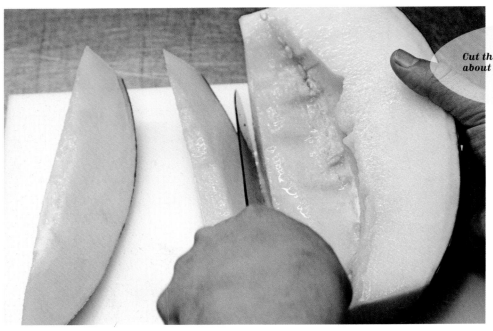

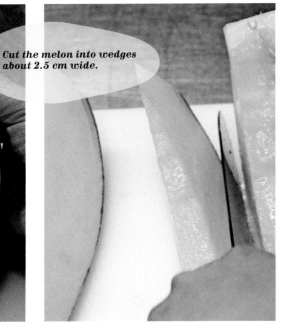

Cut the melon into wedges about 2.5 cm wide.

340

You will need around 2 slices per person.

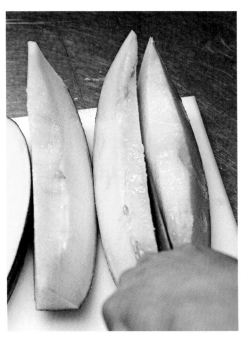

Place the melon wedges on a serving dish.

Place the ham slices on another seving dish.

Serve the ham and melon separately.

Rice with duck

We use sofrito and picada in many rice dishes. Make batches ahead of time and freeze in small quantities, ready for use.

•

With this rice dish, the texture should be creamy.

	for 2	for 6	for 20	for 75
Chicken stock (see page 57)	750 ml	2 l	6 l	22 l
Duck legs	1	3	4 kg	16 kg
Olive oil	2 tbsp	50 ml	130 ml	450 ml
White wine	1½ tbsp	50 ml	130 ml	450 ml
Sofrito (see page 43)	1½ tbsp	180 g	330 g	1 kg
Paella rice	200 g	600 g	2 kg	6.5 kg
Picada (see page 41)	2 tsp	2 tbsp	120 g	400 g

Start →

Put the stock into a saucepan and bring to a simmer.

Meanwhile, cut any excess fat and skin off the duck legs.

Cut the meat into 2.5-cm pieces.

Heat the oil in a large pan over a medium heat. Season the duck with salt, then add to the pan.

Fry the duck for 4–5 minutes, or until deep golden brown.

Pour in the white wine, then loosen any sediment from the bottom of the pan with a wooden spoon.

When most of the wine has boiled away, add the sofrito.

Cook for 5 minutes, stirring.

Add the rice to the pan and cook for 3 minutes, stirring all the time.

Pour in the hot stock and cook the rice for 17 minutes, stirring frequently to prevent sticking.

Add the picada to the pan.

Season with salt and pepper.

Remove the pan from the heat and allow the rice and duck to stand for 3 minutes. The rice should be creamy but still with a little bite.

Serve in bowls.

Chocolate cake

There are many types of cake moulds on the market. We recommend flexible silicone moulds so you can be sure that your cake will not stick. If you only have metal moulds, grease them well with butter before use. For this recipe, use circular moulds about 12 cm in diameter and 4 cm deep.

•

This cake should be served lukewarm. We do not recommend making less than the quantity given for 6 people. Any leftover cakes will keep in an airtight container for up to 2 days.

	for 2	for 6	for 20	for 75
Dark chocolate, 60% cocoa	-	175 g	600 g	2.25 kg
Butter, at room temperature	-	90 g	300 g	1.1 kg
Egg whites	-	120 g (4 eggs)	400 g	1.4 kg
Sugar	-	2 tbsp	100 g	300 g
Egg yolks	-	15 g (1½ eggs)	50 g	175 g

Start →

Chop the chocolate into small pieces.

Half-fill a saucepan with water and place over a low heat, then sit a metal or glass bowl over the pan so that the bottom of the bowl does not touch the water. Put the chocolate into the bowl.

Leave the chocolate to melt slowly, stirring occasionally with a spatula until smooth. Remove the pan from the heat.

Cut the butter into cubes and add to the hot chocolate.

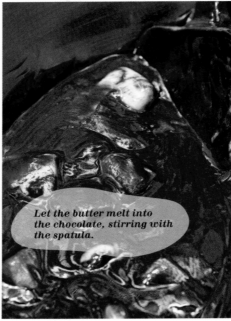

Let the butter melt into the chocolate, stirring with the spatula.

Put the egg whites into a large bowl, then add the sugar. Use a balloon whisk or electric beater to whip the whites and sugar to a soft meringue. Do not allow the mixture to stiffen.

Preheat the oven to 200°C/ 400°F/Gas Mark 6.

Continue →

In a separate bowl, whisk the egg yolks for a few seconds.

Pour the yolks over the meringue mixture, then fold together using a spatula or whisk.

Tip the meringue mixture into the buttery chocolate.

Fold everything together carefully with a spatula until even.

Spoon the cake mixture into a piping bag and snip off the end. If you don't have a piping bag, use two teaspoons instead.

Pipe or carefully spoon the mixture into circular silicone moulds about 12 cm across and 4 cm deep.

Bake in the oven for 12 minutes, or until risen and shrinking away from the edges of the moulds.

Leave to cool a little before removing from the moulds.

Serve the cakes warm.

–

Meal 29

–

Roasted vegetables with olive oil

–

Salmon stewed with lentils

–

White chocolate cream

INGREDIENTS

BUY FRESH
* large aubergines
* large red peppers
* fresh salmon fillet
* fresh parsley
* cooked lentils
* shelled pistachios
* onions

IN THE CUPBOARD
* olive oil
* salt
* sherry vinegar
* black peppercorns
* white chocolate

IN THE FRIDGE
* eggs
* whipping cream,
  35% fat

IN THE FREEZER
* sofrito
  (see page 43)
* fish stock
  (see page 56)
* picada
  (see page 41)

348

ORGANIZING THE MENU

	Hours before the meal
	4
	3½
	3
	2½
	2
1½ hours before _____	1½
Roast the vegetables, then leave to cool	
1 hour before _____	1
Make the white chocolate cream and chill in the fridge	
45 minutes before _____	
Prepare the salmon and parsley for the lentils	½
15 minutes before _____	
Start cooking the lentils	
10 minutes before _____	
Dress the vegetables with the vinaigrette	
Just before eating _____	
Add the salmon to the lentils	
_____	Start of the meal
Just before dessert _____	
Sprinkle the pistachios over the white chocolate cream	
_____	Dessert

Roasted vegetables with olive oil

In Spain this dish is called *escalivada*. The name comes from the Catalan verb *escalivar*, which means to cook in hot ashes. It refers to a dish of vegetables roasted with olive oil.

•

If you do not have enough juices left from roasting the vegetables to make a vinaigrette, add more sherry vinegar and olive oil.

	for 2	for 6	for 20	for 75
Large aubergines	1	3	2 kg	7.5 kg
Large red peppers	1	3	2 kg	7.5 kg
Olive oil	2 tbsp	6 tbsp	300 g	1 kg
Salt	1 pinch	2 pinches	25 g	100 g
Medium onions	2	6	2 kg	7.5 kg
For the vinaigrette:				
Sherry vinegar	1 tsp	1 tbsp	30 ml	100 ml
Olive oil	2 tbsp	6 tbsp	300 ml	1 l
Salt	1 pinch	2 pinches	15 g	40 g

Start →

Preheat the oven to 200°C/400°F/Gas Mark 6.

Put the aubergines and peppers into a roasting tin, drizzle with the oil and sprinkle with the salt.

Wrap the onions in aluminium foil and add to the tin. Roast the vegetables all together for 45 minutes.

After 45 minutes, the pepper skins will be blackened and the aubergines very soft. Leave until cool enough to handle. Keep any juices that have collected in the pan.

Peel the skin from the peppers and remove the seeds.

Cut the stalks from the aubergines, then peel them.

Continue →

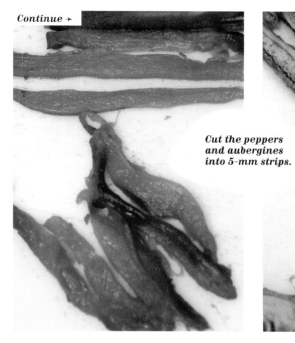

Cut the peppers and aubergines into 5-mm strips.

Unwrap the onions, peel away the skins, then cut the flesh into quarters. Again, set aside any juices released during cooking.

Arrange the vegetables in separate piles on a serving dish.

Make a vinaigrette by mixing any juice from the vegetables with the sherry vinegar and oil.

Season with salt.

Dress the vegetables with the vinaigrette and serve.

Salmon stewed with lentils

Ask your fishmonger to clean, gut and skin the fish for you if you prefer.

•

This dish is also good with other types of oily fish, such as mackerel. To make it with shellfish, use small round clams, small razor clams or mussels.

	for 2	for 6	for 20	for 75
Fresh salmon fillet	300 g	900 g	3 kg	12 kg
Fresh parsley	2 tsp	2 tbsp	1 bunch	3 bunches
Olive oil	2 tsp	2 tbsp	50 ml	200 ml
Sofrito (see page 43)	1 tbsp	3 tbsp	300 g	1 kg
Fish stock (see page 56)	400 ml	1.2 l	3.5 l	10 l
Tinned lentils, drained	300 g	900 g	3 kg	10 kg
Picada (see page 41)	2 tsp	2 tbsp	150 g	400 g
Salt	A pinch	2 pinches	3 g	10 g

Start →

Remove the skin from the salmon fillet.

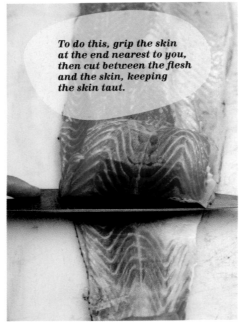

To do this, grip the skin at the end nearest to you, then cut between the flesh and the skin, keeping the skin taut.

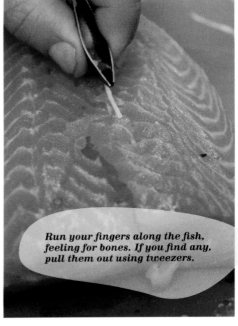

Run your fingers along the fish, feeling for bones. If you find any, pull them out using tweezers.

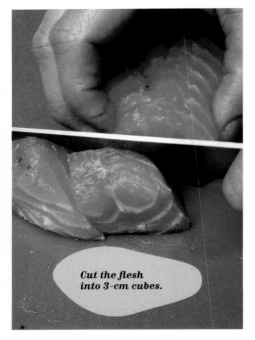

Cut the flesh into 3-cm cubes.

You will need 10 pieces per serving.

Pick the parsley leaves from the stems.

Continue →

Chop it finely.

Place a saucepan over a medium heat, then pour in the oil and add the sofrito.

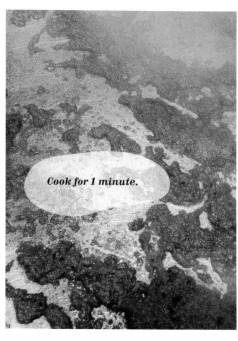

Cook for 1 minute.

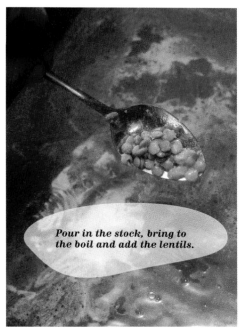

Pour in the stock, bring to the boil and add the lentils.

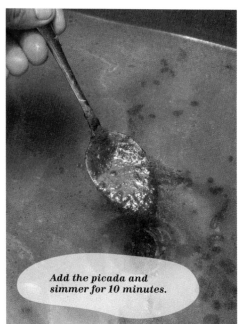

Add the picada and simmer for 10 minutes.

Season the salmon with salt and add to the pan.

After 1 minute, turn the salmon in the pan, taking care not to break it up, then season to taste with more salt if needed.

Sprinkle the chopped parsley into the pan and carefully stir in.

Serve the stew in shallow bowls.

White chocolate cream

We serve this topped with toasted pistachios, but they can be substituted with other toasted nuts, or fresh or freeze-dried raspberries or strawberries.

•

To toast the pistachios, put them in a frying pan over a medium-high heat and cook for 2 minutes, stirring continuously until golden.

•

The white chocolate cream can be made the day before you want to eat it.

	for 2	for 6	for 20	for 75
White chocolate	70 g	220 g	800 g	3.63 kg
Whipping cream, 35% fat	90 ml	260 ml	1.42 l	4.28 l
Egg yolks	1	3	220 g	990 g
Shelled, toasted pistachios	20 g	100 g	150 g	670 g

Start →

Finely chop the white chocolate.

Pour the cream into a saucepan and bring to the boil.

Whisk the egg yolks in a large bowl, then pour in the hot cream, whisking continuously.

Pour the mixture back into a clean pan, place over a low heat, then cook for about 3 minutes, stirring continuously, until just thickened. Do not allow to boil.

Continue →

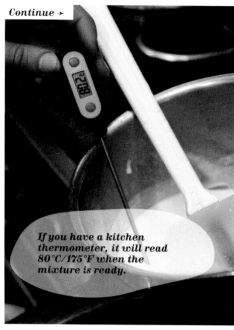

If you have a kitchen thermometer, it will read 80°C/175°F when the mixture is ready.

Pour the hot mixture over the chocolate and leave to melt for 2 minutes.

Whisk to make a smooth cream.

Ladle into bowls, then chill for 1 hour until firm.

Sprinkle the pistachios over the top of the cream before serving.

–

Meal 30

–

Grilled lettuce hearts

–

Veal with red wine & mustard

–

Chocolate mousse

INGREDIENTS

BUY FRESH
* fresh mint
* lettuce hearts
* veal cheeks

IN THE CUPBOARD
* sherry vinegar
* wholegrain mustard
* olive oil
* salt
* black peppercorns
* brandy
* red wine
* sugar
* instant potato flakes
* dark chocolate,
  60% cocoa
* N_2O cartridges
  for the siphon
* caramelized
  hazelnuts

IN THE FRIDGE
* eggs
* whole milk
* butter
* whipping cream,
  35% fat

ORGANIZING THE MENU

	Hours before the meal
	4
3½ hours before _____	3½
Brown and cook the veal cheeks (if using the oven method)	
	3
	2½
	2
	1½
1 hour before _____	1
Brown and cook the veal cheeks (if using a pressure cooker)	
Make the chocolate mousse mix and fill the siphon	½
20 minutes before _____	__
Make the vinaigrette and cut the lettuce hearts	
10 minutes before _____	__
Make the mashed potato	
Just before eating _____	Start of the meal
Cook the lettuce hearts and dress with the vinaigrette	
Just before main course __ __	
Reduce the veal cheek sauce _____	Main course
Just before dessert _____ __	
Dispense the chocolate mousse and sprinkle with the hazelnuts _____	
	Dessert

Grilled lettuce hearts

When making the vinaigrette,
it is important not to let it emulsify,
so do not over-whisk it.

•

If lettuce hearts are not available,
use endive instead.

	for 2	for 6	for 20	for 75
Sprigs fresh mint	8	20 g	33 g	100 g
Wholegrain mustard	1 tsp	1 tbsp	180 g	570 g
Sherry vinegar	1 tbsp	3 tbsp	110 ml	335 ml
Egg yolks	1	3	8	25
Olive oil, plus extra for frying	6 tbsp	240 ml	900 ml	2.7 l
Lettuce hearts, such as Little Gem	2	6	20	75

Start →

To make the dressing, put
the mint leaves and mustard
into a tall jug or beaker.

Add the sherry vinegar.

Add the egg yolk.

Continue →

Add the oil while processing with a hand-held blender until the mint is finely chopped. Season with salt.

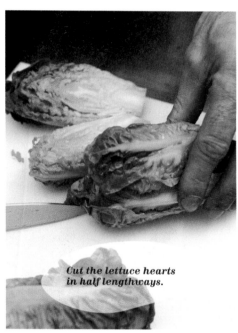

Cut the lettuce hearts in half lengthways.

Heat a large frying pan over a medium heat and add a little oil. Season the lettuce hearts with salt, then fry for about 5 minutes until golden on both sides.

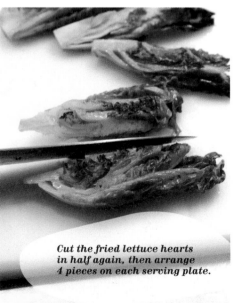

Cut the fried lettuce hearts in half again, then arrange 4 pieces on each serving plate.

Pour the mint vinaigrette over the lettuce just before serving.

Veal with red wine & mustard

A pressure cooker is ideal for cooking veal cheeks quickly. If you do not have one, this recipe can easily be made in the oven. Preheat the oven to 180°C/350°F/Gas Mark 4. Brown the cheeks in a casserole, add the liquids, then cover and cook for 3 hours, until very tender, then finish with the mustard.

•

This dish can be made with pork cheeks or other cuts suitable for slow cooking, such as veal or beef shank or shin.

	for 2	for 6	for 20	for 75
Veal cheeks	2	6	20	75
Olive oil	2 tsp	1½ tbsp	200 ml	500 ml
Brandy	3 tbsp	100 ml	500 ml	1.5 l
Red wine	500 ml	1 l	3 l	9 l
Sugar	2 tsp	1½ tbsp	80 g	200 g
Water	1 l	2 l	4 l	12 l
Wholegrain mustard	1 tsp	1½ tbsp	60 g	250 g
Whole milk	200 ml	500 ml	2.5 l	7.5 l
Butter	10 g	25 g	250 g	750 g
Instant potato flakes	25 g	65 g	300 g	930 g

Start →

Season the veal cheeks with salt and pepper.

Put the base of your pressure cooker over a medium heat, add the oil and then the veal cheeks. Brown well on each side.

If you are cooking more than 2 cheeks, brown them in batches and set aside on a plate.

Return the veal cheeks to the pan, pour in the brandy and let it reduce a little.

Add the sugar and pour in the wine.

Continue →

Once the wine has reduced and looks syrupy, add the water.

Add the mustard.

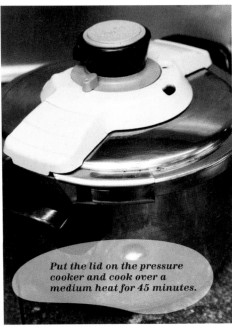

Put the lid on the pressure cooker and cook over a medium heat for 45 minutes.

Meanwhile, make the creamed potatoes. Bring the milk to the boil and add the butter.

Add the potato flakes and cook, stirring, until thickened.

Blend to a smooth purée with a hand-held blender or whisk. Season with salt and pepper.

Remove the lid and simmer the sauce until thickened and glossy.

Serve the veal cheeks whole, covered with the wine and mustard sauce, and with a dish of creamed potatoes on the side.

Chocolate mousse

The minimum quantity of mousse you can make using a siphon is 6–8 portions. If you do not have a siphon, you could whisk the egg whites to stiff peaks and fold them through the chocolate mixture, although the texture will be very different.

•

Any kind of crunchy, nutty topping, such as crushed almond or peanut brittle, can be substituted for the caramelized hazelnuts.

	for 2	for 6-8	for 20	for 75
Dark chocolate, 60% cocoa	–	130 g	640 g	2.4 kg
Whipping cream, 35% fat	–	120 ml	600 g	2.2 kg
Egg whites	–	4	450 g	1.7 kg
N$_2$O cartridges for the siphon	–	1	3	8
Caramelized hazelnuts	–	30	300 g	1 kg

For 6–8 people, use a 0.5-litre siphon. For the larger quantities use 1-litre siphons.

Start →

Finely chop the chocolate and put into a bowl.

Pour the cream into a saucepan, set over a high heat, then bring to the boil.

Pour the boiling cream over the chocolate.

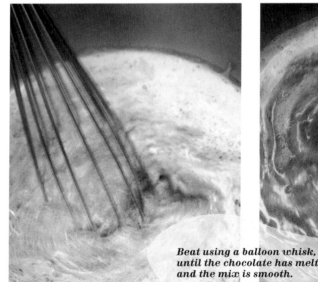

Beat using a balloon whisk, until the chocolate has melted and the mix is smooth.

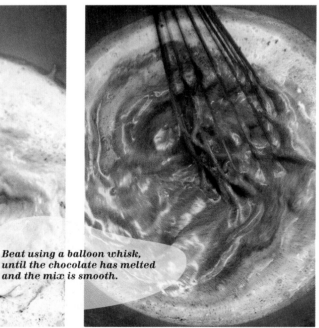

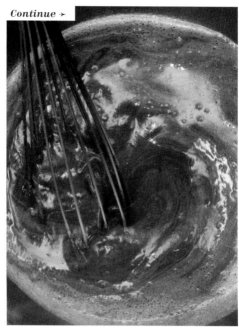

Set aside to cool a little.

Add the egg whites and stir until thoroughly combined.

Pass the mixture through a fine-meshed sieve, then pour into the siphon.

Seal the top, then charge the siphon with the cartridge.

Shake the siphon vigorously, then set aside at room temperature until needed.

Dispense the mousse into small bowls or glasses.

Top with the caramelized hazelnuts or your chosen topping.

Waldorf salad

–

Noodle soup with mussels

–

Melon & mint soup with pink grapefruit

INGREDIENTS

BUY FRESH
* celery
* lemons
* Golden Delicious
  apples
* small mussels
* large ripe melon, such
  as cantaloupe or *piel
  de sapo*
* pink grapefruit
* fresh mint

IN THE CUPBOARD
* walnut halves
* wholegrain mustard
* salt
* black peppercorns
* filini pasta
* olive oil
* white wine
* sugar

IN THE FRIDGE
* whipping cream,
  35% fat
* mayonnaise

IN THE FREEZER
* fish stock
  (see page 56)
* sofrito (see page 43)
* picada (see page 41)

ORGANIZING THE MENU

	Hours before the meal
	4
	3½
	3
	2½
	2
	1½
1 hour before Make the melon soup and segment and then chill the grapefruit	1
Clean the mussels and return to the fridge	
30 minutes before Bring the stock to a simmer	½
Make the salad dressing	
Chop the celery, apple and walnuts	
20 minutes before Start cooking the pasta	
10 minutes before Add the sofrito, wine, stock and picada to the pasta	
Finish preparing the salad	
Just before eating Add the mussels to the soup	
	Start of the meal
Just before dessert Put the grapefruit into bowls, then ladle over the melon soup	
	Dessert

Waldorf salad

When making a large amount
of salad, we toss the apple
in ascorbic acid (vitamin C powder)
to prevent the flesh from browning.
You can use lemon juice
to the same effect.

	for 2	for 6	for 20	for 75
Celery	100 g	300 g	1 kg	3.5 kg
Walnut halves	30 g	90 g	300 g	1 kg
Mayonnaise	60 g	180 g	600 g	2 kg
Wholegrain mustard	2 tsp	1½ tbsp	65 g	225 g
Whipping cream, 35% fat	1½ tbsp	4 tbsp	150 g	500 g
Golden Delicious apples	1	3	7	25
Lemon juice, strained	1 tbsp	2 tbsp	75 ml	280 ml

Start →

Trim away the celery leaves, then de-string by peeling with a vegetable peeler.

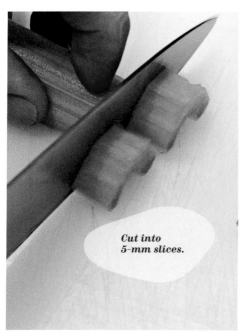

Cut into 5-mm slices.

Break the walnut halves in two.

For the dressing, put the mayonnaise into a bowl, then stir in the mustard.

Continue →

Stir in the cream and lemon juice, then season with salt.

Peel the apples.

Cut the apple flesh away from the core.

Cut into small cubes about 1 cm across.

Mix the celery, apple and walnuts in a salad bowl.

Spoon in the dressing and stir well until everything is well coated. Season the salad with salt and pepper.

Serve in small bowls.

Noodle soup with mussels

Sometimes we like to add paprika or saffron to this dish.

•

Baby clams can be used instead of mussels, and any short spaghetti-like pasta can be used instead of filini.

•

Keeping batches of fish stock, sofrito and picada ready in the freezer makes this (and many other dishes) simple and quick to make.

	for 2	for 6	for 20	for 75
Small mussels	115 g	350 g	2.25 kg	8.5 kg
Fish stock (see page 56)	400 ml	1.2 l	4.5 l	16 l
Olive oil	2 tsp	4 tbsp	200 ml	700 ml
Filini pasta	180 g	540 g	1.8 kg	7 kg
Sofrito (see page 43)	30 g	90 g	300 g	1 kg
White wine	1½ tbsp	4 tbsp	150 ml	500 ml
Picada (see page 41)	2 tsp	1½ tbsp	120 g	400 g

Start →

Scrub, then de-beard the mussels under cold running water.

Put the stock into a saucepan and bring to a simmer.

Heat the oil in a large pan, then add the pasta.

Fry the pasta for 1–2 minutes, or until golden.

Add the sofrito to the pasta and cook for 2 minutes.

Stir well.

Continue →

Pour in the wine, loosening the sediment from the bottom of the pan.

Add the hot stock and then the picada. Boil for 10 minutes.

Drop the mussels into the soup, cover the pan and simmer for 5 minutes.

The mussels are ready when they have opened up completely. Discard any that have stayed shut.

Remove the pan from the heat, season with salt and pepper, and serve.

Melon & mint soup with pink grapefruit

We do not recommend making a smaller quantity than that given for 6 people. Any leftover soup makes a delicious alternative to your fruit juice at breakfast the next day. Store it in the fridge overnight.

•

Cantaloupe or *piel de sapo* (toad skin) melons are good for this recipe. If the melon is ripe, the ends will yield slightly when pressed.

	for 2	for 6	for 20	for 75
Large ripe melon	-	1	3	10
Fresh mint leaves	-	10	20 g	70 g
Pink grapefruit	-	2	1.5 kg	5 kg
Sugar	-	2 tbsp	150 g	500 g

Start →

Cut the ends off the melon and slice in half.

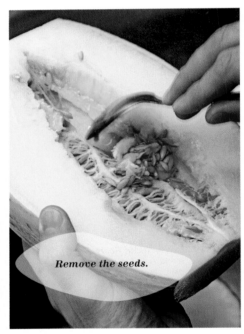

Remove the seeds.

Slice each half into wedges, then remove the skin.

Cut each wedge into pieces.

Purée the melon with a hand-held blender or food processor to make a soup.

Continue →

Pick the mint leaves off the stems, reserving a few for the garnish.

Add the mint leaves, blend until smooth, then add the sugar and repeat.

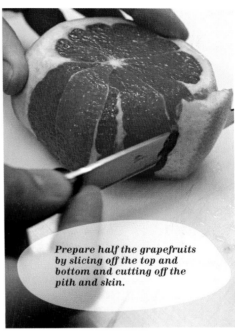

Prepare half the grapefruits by slicing off the top and bottom and cutting off the pith and skin.

Remove the flesh from each segment and set aside.

Squeeze the remaining grapefruit.

Pour the juice into the soup and stir it in.

Strain the soup through a fine sieve.

To serve, put a few grapefruit segments in the bottom of each bowl, then add a few sprigs of mint.

Pour the soup over the grapefruit and serve.

Glossary & Index

Glossary

ACHIOTE PASTE
A paste made from achiote (also known as annatto) seeds that come from the achiote shrub, which is common in South America.

BROWN
To pan-fry ingredients in very hot fat in order to colour the surface.

BRAISE
To cook gently in a sealed pot with stock or thick sauce.

BLANCH
To cook briefly in boiling water. Usually followed by plunging straight into cold water to stop further cooking.

CARAMELIZE
To cook until golden, and the point at which the natural sugars begin to turn to caramel. A blowtorch is often used to caramelize the top of a custard.

CHANTILLY
A classic French preparation of cream whipped with sugar.

COAT
To cover a dish with a substance, such as a sauce.

CREAM
To beat eggs or butter and sugar together with a whisk or wooden spoon until they become thick and pale in colour.

CRU
Denotes a procedure in which a solid substance is infused with a liquid, thus absorbing its flavour.

COUSCOUS
Tiny semolina pellets that have been rolled and coated with wheat flour.

DRAIN
To remove the liquid from a food, usually by tipping into a sieve or colander.

DRIZZLE
To pour a small amount of liquid over a surface.

EMULSIFY
To mix liquids of different densities to form a thicker liquid.

FOLD
To mix food gently from the bottom of the bowl to the top. A large metal spoon or spatula is best for this.

GREMOLATA
A chopped herb condiment made with lemon, garlic and parsley, often served with ossobuco.

GUT
To remove the entrails of a fish.

MARCONA ALMONDS
A sweet-flavoured Spanish variety of almond.

MARINATE
To place raw meat or other foods in an aromatic liquid in order to tenderize prior to cooking, or to add extra flavour.

MISE EN PLACE
The culinary procedures and preparations that take place in a restaurant kitchen before service begins, such as preparing sauces and chopping vegetables.

N_2O CARTRIDGE
A steel cylinder that is filled with nitrous oxide. A cartridge charges the siphon.

PAELLA RICE
A short-grained, thick type of rice often used in Spain. Bomba is the best-known variety.

PLANCHADA BEANS
Long white beans typical of Spain. When cooked they have a smooth creamy texture.

POACH
To cook gently in a liquid such as water, stock or milk.

PROCESS
To mix thoroughly with a blender or electric mixer.

PURÉE
To reduce ingredients to a smooth paste in a food processor or blender. Can also be the name given to the paste itself.

QUENELLE
A small portion of food shaped with two spoons into an elongated sphere like a rugby ball.

RONER
A machine used in professional kitchens to poach foods for long periods at a constant low temperature.

RAS EL HANOUT
A classic spice mixture used in Moroccan cuisine. Typically includes cardamom, clove, cinnamon, peppercorn, chili peppers, coriander and turmeric.

REDUCE
To boil or simmer a liquid to evaporate the water it contains, thereby concentrating the flavour and thickening it.

SALT COD
Cod that is packed in salt and dried in order to preserve it. It is said the whiter the cod, the better the quality.

SECOND STOCK
The liquid that results from re-boiling the discarded meat from a stock. It can be used as the base for a new stock to intensify the flavour.

SHAOXING RICE WINE
China's best-known rice wine, made from fermented rice, millet and yeast. Available in Asian speciality shops.

SHICHIMI TOGARASHI
A mix of seven spices used in
Japanese cooking and characterized
by its hot flavour.

SIEVE
A kitchen utensil that separates food
substances through a fine mesh or net.

SIMMER
To cook slowly over a gentle heat,
before the liquid comes to the boil.

SIPHON
Utensil designed to whip cream and
which, in the mid-1990s, enabled the
creation of foams at elBulli.

SKIM
To remove the frothy scum from
the surface of a liquid using a ladle
or large spoon.

SPRIG
A small shoot or twig from a plant or
herb.

STAGE
A temporary work experience
placement in a restaurant (those
participating are known as 'stagers').

STEAM
To cook in a perforated container
set over boiling water with a tight-
fitting lid.

STOCK
A flavoured cooking liquid obtained
by simmering beef, pork, poultry
or fish with vegetables and aromatics
in water.

THAI CURRY PASTE
A blend of herbs, chillies, and other
aromatic ingredients used as a base
for Thai curries, and available in three
colours: red, green and yellow.

THICKEN
To add ingredients, such as egg yolks or
flour, to make a sauce or soup thicker.

TRIM
To remove all of the inedible or
blemished parts from food.

VACUUM PACK
A method of packaging or storing food
in an airless environment. Often
used in professional kitchens.

VINO RANCIO
A Spanish fortified wine similar in
flavour to sherry.

VIOLIN
The elBulli term for large oval platters
upon which the family meals are
served.

WHISK
To beat rapidly with a flexible tool
to increase the volume and aerate
the ingredients.

ZEST
The thin outer layer of a citrus fruit,
on top of the white pith. Usually grated.

Index

Recipe notes

All herbs are fresh, unless otherwise specified.

Parsley is flat-leaf parsley.

All flour is plain white flour, unless otherwise specified.

All sugar is white caster sugar, unless otherwise specified.

Eggs are medium size, butter is unsalted, and milk is full cream, unless otherwise specified.

Cooking times and temperatures are for guidance only, as individual ovens vary. If using a fan oven, follow the manufacturer's instructions to adjust the oven temperatures as necessary.

Exercise caution when following recipes involving any potentially hazardous activity, including the use of high temperatures, open flames and when deep frying. In particular, when deep frying, add food carefully to avoid splashing, wear long sleeves and never leave the pan unattended.

Some recipes include raw or very lightly cooked eggs, fish or meat. These should be avoided by the elderly, infants, pregnant women, convalescents and anyone with an impaired immune system.

All spoon measurements are level unless otherwise stated. Australian standard tablespoons are 20 ml. Australian readers are advised to use 3 teaspoons in place of 1 tablespoon when measuring small quantities. 1 teaspoon = 5 ml, 1 tablespoon = 15 ml.

Phaidon Press Limited
Regent's Wharf
All Saints Street
London N1 9PA

www.phaidon.com

© 2011 Phaidon Press Limited

ISBN: 9 780 7148 6239 2
(UK edition)

A CIP catalogue for this book is available
from the British Library.

Commissioning Editor: Emilia Terragni
Project Editors: Meredith Erickson and
Laura Gladwin
Production Controller: Marina Asenjo

Designed by Julia Hasting
Photography by Francesc Guillamet and
Maribel Ruiz de Erenchun

Printed in Italy

The Publisher would like to thank Ferran
Adrià for his commitment and enthusiasm;
Marc Cuspinera, Josep Maria Pinto and
the entire staff at elBulli for all their hard
work and assistance; and Hans Stofregen
and Sophie Hodgkin for their contributions
to the book.